PRAISE FOR *IS GOD IS*

"Reinvents *The Good, the Bad and the Ugly* . . . Step aside, Quentin Tarantino and Martin McDonagh, and all you other macho purveyors of mutilation and mayhem with a smile. A snarly new master of high-octane carnage has risen into view. And she—yes, she—is putting her own audacious stamp on that most venerable of pop genres, the old-as-time tale in which getting even comes accessorized with flames, screams, and buckets of blood . . . A gratifying, lurid play."

—BEN BRANTLEY, *NEW YORK TIMES*

"According to the author, this epic 'takes its cues from the ancient, the modern, the tragic, the Spaghetti Western, hip-hop, and Afropunk.' There's hints of *The Oresteia* in there, right alongside *Kill Bill* . . . Harris's play is a rich, funny, unnerving, exhilarating gold mine."

—SARA HOLDREN, *VULTURE*

"*Is God Is* is a language play, in the best of ways . . . there is an intentional performativity that allows the language to exist parallel to, while still driving, the action. The words live in our brains, the action in our stomachs. They meet with every not-so-rhetorical gut-punch."

—DAN O'NEIL, *EXEUNT NYC*

PRAISE FOR *WHAT TO SEND UP WHEN IT GOES DOWN*

"From the start, Harris makes clear that she wrote the play for Black people, and the audience participation is guaranteed to make some viewers uncomfortable. So be it: This is theater as art, exorcism, balm, and battle cry."

—ELISABETH VINCENTELLI, *NEW YORKER*

"*What to Send Up When It Goes Down* will rock you to your core. This electric, uncompromising, and powerfully moving work casts a light on racialized violence and its victims that is both searing and illuminating. Harris has created a play that leaps across categories, registering as part theater piece and part ritual of mourning, remembrance, and resolve."

—DON AUCOIN, *BOSTON GLOBE*

"Go to this show. Go with an open mind and an open heart and quiet mouth and ego and be prepared to be granted a look into the reality of Black lives. It will make a difference in how you see."

—MARY ANN JOHNSON, *MD THEATRE GUIDE*

"There are two concentric parts to Aleshea Harris's part-ceremony, part-play . . . The center of the night is Harris's vivid choreopoem, an intertwined series of short scenes that include song, dance, and absurdist microplays. It's as though Harris had taken her artistic forebear's Ntozake Shange's loose-woven theatrical fabric and stretched it into something tighter and crisper, capable of resounding like a struck drumhead."

—HELEN SHAW, *TIME OUT NEW YORK*

"'An anger spittoon.' The phrase crackles with both a deep visceral charge and an elegant precision. These words are only three among many used by the playwright Aleshea Harris to characterize her truly sui generis, truly remarkable work, *What to Send Up When It Goes Down* . . . Ms. Harris has a gift for pushing the familiar to surreally logical extremes."

—BEN BRANTLEY, *NEW YORK TIMES*

"*Is God Is*, a tragicomic account of African-American sisters tasked by their mother with avenging their father, was one of last season's most exciting and darkly thrilling new works. While *What to Send Up* affirms Harris's gifts as a storyteller and weaver of words, it is, as you'd expect, markedly different in structure and intent, packing the kind of emotional wallop that only the truth can deliver."

—ELYSA GARDNER, *NEW YORK STAGE REVIEW*

"Even though the actors tell you that the rituals of *What to Send Up When It Goes Down* are primarily for Black audience members, people of any color can—yes, I think, must—relate to the anguish flowing through this intense and edifying experience."

—PETER MARKS, *WASHINGTON POST*

"In *What to Send Up When It Goes Down*, collective rage in response to racialized violence in America is welcomed like a new-born baby, a treasured expression of endearment and a truth that holds the key to empowerment . . . The ritual of release and healing in *What to Send Up When It Goes Down* is the first time I have ever been in a theatrical space that so directly confronts the deep emotions connected to racial victimization—and made it okay to completely express what you always wanted to say but couldn't or wouldn't. In *What to Send Up When It Goes Down*—you can. This feels both frightening and freeing at the same time. What a different feeling for theater. To immerse myself as a participant in the pain, violence, injustice, fear, anger, and disbelief in which so many victims have died at the hands of people who feared them enough to want to destroy them . . . Through a series of three parodied vignettes, *What to Send Up When It Goes Down* escalates in emotions that ascend to heights that honor those who have fallen victim to racialized violence, stirring up waves of fury that crest in overwhelming pain but fall upon calm shores that anchor the joy of overcoming."

—RAMONA HARPER, *DC METRO THEATER ARTS*

"The play itself backs up the preamble and ritual with a fine mix of racially tinged, rotating character sketches, step routines, singalongs, and monologues performed by a uniformly excellent cast . . . Knowledge, compassion, and laughter flow through every scene . . . All the sharing and singing and shouting lead to well-earned catharsis."

—ANDRÉ HEREFORD, *METRO WEEKLY*

"There's a lot to digest in the ninety minutes of *What to Send Up* and still more to unpack long after you leave. But that is precisely why the work excels."

—TAMARA BEST, *DAILY BEAST*

"*What to Send Up* is not derivative, but it is a worthy inheritor of a couple of different strands of socially critical theater. This is theater that sets out to do something: Be that heal, expose, purge, condemn, motivate, or all of the above."

—**ALISON WALLS, *EXEUNT NYC***

"Aleshea Harris has not just written a performance in her production, *What to Send Up When It Goes Down*, she has created a space, a community ritual, and the opportunity for Black audience members to breathe."

—**CELINA COLBY, *BAY STATE BANNER***

IS GOD IS

WHAT TO SEND UP WHEN IT GOES DOWN

IS GOD IS

WHAT TO SEND UP WHEN IT GOES DOWN

ALESHEA HARRIS

THEATRE COMMUNICATIONS GROUP NEW YORK 2021

Is God Is / What to Send Up When It Goes Down is published by Theatre Communications Group, Inc., 520 Eighth Avenue, 24th Floor, New York, NY 10018-4156

The publication of *Is God Is / What to Send Up When It Goes Down* by Aleshea Harris, through TCG's Book Program, is made possible in part by the New York State Council on the Arts with the support of the Office of the Governor and the New York State Legislature.

Special thanks to Judith O. Rubin for her generous support of this publication.

TCG books are exclusively distributed to the book trade by Consortium Book Sales and Distribution.

Library of Congress Control Numbers:
2021041753 (print) / 2021041754 (ebook)
ISBN 978-1-55936-963-3 (paperback) / ISBN 978-1-55936-926-8 (epub)
A catalog record for this book is available from the Library of Congress.

Book design and composition by Lisa Govan
Cover design by Mark Melnick
Front cover: © Toyin Ojih Odutola. Courtesy of the artist and Jack Shainman Gallery, New York

First Edition, December 2021

For Ma, who holds us all despite the burning

ACKNOWLEDGMENTS

I owe my thanks to Douglas Kearney, Brian Carbine, Rachel Kauder Nalebuff, Mona Heinze, Automata, Thymele Arts, Taibi Magar, Whitney White, the actors who lent their voices to early drafts, the first folx to bring these plays to light, and Black people, who are the soul and gut of these plays and the only good reason for me to write anything.

CONTENTS

IS GOD IS 1

WHAT TO SEND UP WHEN IT GOES DOWN 125

IS GOD IS

PRODUCTION HISTORY

Is God Is had its world premiere at Soho Rep. (Sarah Benson, Artistic Director; Cynthia Flowers, Executive Director) in New York City, on February 6, 2018. It was directed by Taibi Magar. The scenic design was by Adam Rigg, the costume design was by Montana Levi Blanco, the lighting design was by Matthew Richards, the sound design was by Jeremy Toussaint-Baptiste, and hair and wig design were by Cookie Jordan. The fight choreographer was J. David Brimmer and the production stage manager was Danielle Teague-Daniels. The cast was:

RACINE	Dame-Jasmine Hughes
ANAIA	Alfie Fuller
SHE	Nehassaiu deGannes
CHUCK HALL	Michael Genet
RILEY	Anthony Cason
SCOTCH	Caleb Eberhardt
ANGIE	Nehassaiu deGannes
MAN	Teagle F. Bougere

Is God Is opened at The Royal Court (Vicky Featherstone, Artistic Director; Lucy Davies, Executive Producer) in London, on September 10, 2021. It was directed by Ola Ince. The scenic design was by Chloe Lamford, the costume design was by Natalie Pryce, the lighting design was by Simisola Lucia Majekodunmi, the sound design was by Max Perryment, and the original music was by Renell Shaw. The movement director was Imogen Knight, the choreographer was Jordan 'JFunk' Franklin, and the fight director was Philip d'Orléans. The cast was:

RACINE	Tamara Lawrance
ANAIA	Adelayo Adedayo
SHE	Cecilia Noble
CHUCK HALL	Ray Emmet Brown
RILEY	Rudolphe Mdlongwa
SCOTCH	Ernest Kingsley Jnr
ANGIE	Vivienne Acheampong
MAN	Mark Monero

CHARACTERS—ALL AFRICAN AMERICAN

RACINE A woman of twenty-one years. Identical twin sister to Anaia. Has burn scars on her arms, back and neck, but a face of considerable beauty.

ANAIA Has burn scars on her arms, face and neck. Hard to look at. Wears a wig.

SHE Mother to Racine and Anaia. Has burn scars over her entire body.

CHUCK HALL A lawyer. Middle-aged.

RILEY A boy of sixteen.

SCOTCH A boy of sixteen.

ANGIE Mother to Riley and Scotch.

MAN A father.

NOTES

This epic takes its cues from the ancient, the modern, the tragic, the Spaghetti Western, hip-hop, and Afropunk.

This text also includes adventures in typography.

A LETTER

A blazing inferno. Out of the fire step Anaia and Racine.

A studio apartment in the Northeast.

Anaia rubs the scars on Racine's back with ice as the fire subsides.

RACINE AND ANAIA

Twins.

RACINE

Burnin
Them burnin twins
at home in their apartment
in the Northeast
New York or Hampshire
or Jersey

ANAIA

or
Somethin like that
Somewhere that don't feel right

RACINE AND ANAIA

Twins

RACINE

Racine is the rough one who still got some pretty to her.
She only got the scars on her back and a bit creeping up the rear of her neck. You can barely see 'em.

ANAIA

Anaia wasn't so lucky. Face look like it melted and then froze. Mostly people don't let their eyes meet hers.

RACINE

'Cine used the handle of a rake to shut Tommy Danson up in the seventh grade when he called 'Naia a bad name.
Thas the kinda roughness she got.

ANAIA

'Naia is trapped in a prison of sweetness. Girl so ugly don't get to be mean

RACINE

'Cine does though. She got both their mean.
(To Anaia) Got somethin today.

ANAIA

'Naia's too tired for this.
She work in a warehouse packing cold things into boxes all day
She's too tired for this—

RACINE

In the mail. Got somethin. News.

ANAIA

'Naia keep her head down out of habit.
O, yeah? I got news, too.

RACINE

This big, tho.
Got a letter with some news in it. Big news.

ANAIA

Letter from who?

RACINE

From
Mama.

ANAIA

From who?

RACINE

From Mama.

ANAIA

Who Mama?

RACINE

Our Mama.

ANAIA

We got a mama?

RACINE

We do.

ANAIA

Too tired for this
I thought she was dead.

RACINE

Well. She ain't.

ANAIA

I thought she was dead in a fire. Same fire that put these marks on us.

RACINE

Well, she ain't.

ANAIA

Well, what she want? Where she been?

RACINE

You gettin all worked up. Switch.

(Anaia sits. Racine rubs ice on Anaia's scars.)

She wanna see us. She been in a place.
A place for sick people who old.

ANAIA

Uh old folks' home?

RACINE

I think so.

(Takes an envelope from her pocket, reads:)

"Folsom Rest Home for the Weary
2115 Pluckum Drive
Oscarville, Mississippi, Alabama, Florida, Texas, Tennessee, Arkansas, Kentucky
Dirty South 39582313650849."

ANAIA

Thas where she at?

RACINE

Eyup.

ANAIA

Damn. Thas where she been at?

RACINE

Seem like it.

ANAIA

Damn.

RACINE

Hey Twin.

ANAIA

Yeah?

RACINE

Seem like we got to go to where she at.

ANAIA

Go?

RACINE

Yeah.

ANAIA

But we don't know her and she don't know us.

RACINE

She know our names and she knew how to find us.
We got to go see her.

ANAIA

Well, why she ain't come see us in all these years? Ask about us?

RACINE

Only one way to find out. Les go.

ANAIA

Now?

RACINE

Eyup. Right now 'cause she finna go.

ANAIA

Where she finna go?

RACINE

Die.

ANAIA

Die?

RACINE

Eyup. Says so in the letter.

ANAIA

Damn, 'Cine.

RACINE

I know it.

ANAIA

She only wrote to you? She ain't write me?

RACINE

Ain't but my name on the envelope, but she talk about you.

ANAIA

Why she ain't write me?

RACINE

Maybe 'cause she knew you'd be all emotional.

ANAIA

Me?

RACINE

Yeah, you. Even though she ain't been around us she prolly got uh intuition about it. Mamas be knowin 'bout stuff like that.
She can prolly sense how you be gettin all emotional, all sad-sack-y—

ANAIA

I don't be.

RACINE

You do.

ANAIA

Don't.

RACINE

Do. You cried about that kitten we couldn't get outta the engine. The one that died?

ANAIA

It died 'cause you wasn't patient enough to coax it out.

RACINE

Had to get to work. You cried. 'Member? All emotional.

ANAIA

. . . . . . chyeahhhhhh I guess thas true. I do be all emotional sometimes—

RACINE

Like a lil punk.

ANAIA

Yeah, yeah, ha ha—

RACINE

Like a lil bish.

ANAIA

Now you takin it too far.

RACINE

I'm playin.

ANAIA

I got stuff to do, though. I gotta meet up with Ellis and tell him about something—

RACINE

Ellis who?

O. him.

ANAIA

Yeah. We sposed to meet up.

RACINE

'Cine sigh and roll her eyes like,
"Here we go again
'bout that man she met online."

(To Anaia) What you gotta meet up with him for?

ANAIA

We sposed to meet up and talk about the future.

RACINE

'Cine bite her tongue.
(To Anaia) Mhmm.
Switch.

(They switch positions and Anaia is now applying ice to Racine's scars.)

You love him?

ANAIA

No. But I don't want him to leave.

RACINE

Then do what you gotta do to keep him.

ANAIA

He don't like me to look at him when we doin it.

RACINE

So don't look at him. Put your pride away. Some of us don't get to have pride.

ANAIA

True.

RACINE

So, let him get it from behind. If you look at him you might start to catch feelins.

ANAIA

True, true.

RACINE

And we ain't got time for bein weak with feelins for no man, 'Naia.
We got things to do.
She waitin on us.

ANAIA

She finna go, huh?
Go die, huh?

RACINE

Eyup. She finna go so we gotta go.

ANAIA

damn.

RACINE

I
know.

ANAIA

W e l l
I guess I'll catch him later—

RACINE

Thas right. You can catch ol' dude later. We need to look good since this kinda like our first and last time seein her, don't you think? I'm finna dress up. I'm wearin lipstick and all.

ANAIA

I'ma put me on some too.

RACINE

I'm finna get cuuuuuuuute

ANAIA

You don't never get cute. You be on that boho, "I'm-so-pretty-I-ain't-gotta-try" shit.

RACINE

Yeah, but this is Mama
we talkin 'bout.

ANAIA

I feel ya.

(They are both getting pretty-fied.)

That lipstick real red.

RACINE

Eyup.

ANAIA

Like how it feel to know she comin and goin.

ANAIA AND RACINE

You look good. Thanks.
Think she'll like it?
Yeah. Yeah. Yeah.

BEFORE GOD

The twins stand before an immense door.

RACINE

We in it. This is it.
Folsom Rest Home for the Weary.
2115 Pluckum Drive
Oscarville, Mississippi, Alabama, Florida, Texas, Tennessee, Arkansas, Kentucky
Dirty South 39582313650849
Room 416B.
And a sign with our names on it. She musta did that so we'd know we was in the right place.

ANAIA

My name ain't spelt right.

RACINE

O, come on, 'Naia.

ANAIA

You think she still alive?

RACINE

Only one way to find out.

ANAIA

My mascara runnin?

RACINE

A little.

ANAIA

Iss hot.

RACINE

Yeah. Dirty South stay hot.

ANAIA

You ready?

RACINE

To see God?

ANAIA

God?

RACINE

Well, she made us, didn't she?

ANAIA

You gon' get struck down.

SHE

A n ai a? R a c i ne?

(They look at one another.)

That y'all?

ANAIA

You go on in.

RACINE

You first.

SHE

I can f e e l y'all out there.

ANAIA

First born is the first one in.

RACINE

Thas stupid.

SHE

you're wastin you're wastin

time.

(She is wheezing. She lies on her deathbed. She huffs, coughs and struggles to breathe. Her voice comes out in hoarse rasps.)

I'm

so glad

you

could make it.

Had the nurse

put the sign out by my door   a sign with your names on it

see it?

RACINE

Yes, Mama.
We. We
We really liked that sign.
We seen it.

ANAIA

My name ain't spelt right.

SHE

Good. Lemme look at y'all.

(They step closer.)

Okay. I see.
Anaia and Racine.
Used to put y'all in opposite clothes so I could tell you apart.
Anaia you was always in tropical colors and Racine
I had you in pastels. No matchy-matchy for my girls.

RACINE

Thas nice. Now I like tropical and 'Naia like pastels.

ANAIA

Thas a lie.

RACINE

Shut up.
So. How you been?

SHE

(Laughs) O, you know.
Dyin.

RACINE

Yeah, yeah. I see you got them tubes in you.
We came soon as we could. Had to take off work but we here.
I work at a daycare and 'Naia work in a warehouse.
She got a boyfriend.

ANAIA

thas a lie

SHE

She got something else, too.

RACINE

Ma'am?

SHE

Nothin. She quiet.

ANAIA

hi mama.

SHE

I ain't wrote you, 'Naia
'cause you be gettin all emotional.
Been that way since you was little. I know.
I ain't wanna upset you.

ANAIA

I
I know.
Thank you.

SHE

My girls.

RACINE

Yeah.

SHE

My baby girls.

RACINE

Eyup. Thas us.

SHE

Y'all are lookin at The Last Days
I keep tellin myself,
"Ruby, this might be your last Thursday
your last time wakin up in this bed
your last time thinkin iss your last time."

(She laughs. Twins join, nervously.)

Y'all done got so big.

ANAIA

Yeah. Been eighteen years.

SHE

Eyup.

ANAIA

We thought you was dead.

SHE

Thas what I wanted y'all to think.
Who want
a mama
with a body
like uh
a l l i g a t o r ?

ANAIA

Why
why you got a body like uh alligator?

SHE

'Causa what he did.

ANAIA

He who?

SHE

They ain't told y'all.

RACINE

Naw, they just said you was dead.

ANAIA

So we a little confused 'cause you alive but you ain't write us or nothin.

RACINE

But we ain't really worried about all that—

ANAIA

Eighteen years. Been eighteen years.

(An awkward pause.)

SHE

Was that
an awkward pause?

(She laughs. Racine joins, nervously.)

All you know is it was a fire and your mama was gone, huh?

RACINE	ANAIA
Thas pretty much what we been told.	Yeah.

SHE

Well
i'm 'on tell you
there's more.

Had it all sealt up so you could walk without shame
but iss more and you need to know it so you understand your mama ain't just up and leave you
iss more to it than that.

ANAIA

What more?

SHE

I'll tell you It was a regular day. I had took y'all to daycare and went to work. Regular day. Got off work, got y'all and came home, a baby in each arm. Y'all was three.
We get home and I put y'all in the kitchen at the table with some apple slices—a snack while I made dinner.
I had just chopped the onions at the counter
I'll never forget it
just chopped the onions when I heard the window in the bathroom shut.

(A kind of flashback. She retreats into the past, hearing the window, suspicious.)

Hello?
The TV. Cartoons—loud

Hello?

The curtains in the kitchen—breathin. The onion on the cutting board—waitin.
I rinse my hands and wipe 'em on my dress, iss an old dress.

Hello? I pat your baby-heads, go down the hall
Maybe just a branch against the window
Hello?
Only, ain't no trees near our windows
Hello?
Down the hall. Bathroom door wide open. Dark in there.
The mirror showing my scared silhouette. Nothin in here but a bone-tired woman.

(She laughs.)

My hand goes to the light switch
just to be, just to be sure, you know? Can't be too careful
He said he was gon come back, so
Just to be sure
And the green light flashes on
and issa hand on the shower curtain
O god
The fear like an ax to the middle of my chest
O no
His hand, he pull the curtain aside kinda sweet-like and

it reminds me of why I fell in love with him
he do got a tender side
he pull the curtain aside and just stands there
No smile or nothin. No frown, neither. Face as plain as a slice of wheat bread.

"Hey"

He says, like we on the street or somethin
like he ain't just break into my bathroom
like it wasn't no restraining order
I couldn't even scream or nothin

Just

"Hey. You back."

A nod.
My mouth is twitching and my guts is on fire

"The kids are in the kitchen. I was just making dinner—"

And iss like a train runs into my throat
He grips   hard.
That same plain face right up next to mine, barely sweatin and even lookin at me in a tender way
I can hear what sounds like a lullaby just before everything turns dark.

(Sound of a liquid being poured and Man whistling.)

When I come to I smell it. Liquor. Issa sickly sweet smell.

Soaked in it.
Good thing this dress is old
It wouldn't never come out.

And he's whistling like a little bird while he do it.
His boots step all in it. He's whistling and pouring.
Not rushing, just easy. He's gonna kill me easy.
Then the boots are still. Here go. Here go.
I close my eyes

                                   but nothin happens.
A full minute passes—all I hear is my breath and you two in the kitchen giggling like how babies giggle like they got the sun in they mouth   ya know?
And the boots move tward y'all in the kitchen
And I can't talk 'cause he took the wind outta my mouth
but in my throat is a rattle like:

"D o n't y o u f u c k i n g t o u c h m y b a b i e s!!!"

But he already bringin y'all. 'Cine, I think he was holding you. 'Naia, you was walking. One of y'all was sayin
"daddy where you been?"
And he sayin
"on the Moon"
"the mooooon?"
"Yup. With the aliens."
And by now y'all in the bathroom standing over me.
And 'Cine, you wasn't scared. You said to him,
"Daddy . . . whasss wrong with Mommy? What she on the ground for?"
And he said, "Mommy's sleepy and she want us to wake her up. You gonna help me wake her up, Anaia?"
And 'Naia, you was always the emotional one, you could tell somethin was off and you was scared. You say,

"I I wanna I wanna go back and watch Scooby-Doo."
"Just a minute. Let's wake Mommy up."
"How?"
"Like this."

(A sound like a thousand matches being struck simultaneously.)

And 'Naia went to whining.
"daddy i don't like this."
And then he musta dropped that little bit of fire on me 'cause it was all on me gettin bigger, that quick

eatin through me 'til my brain was smart enough to turn off.

Thahwasit.

RACINE

Damn.
Mama. Damn.
We was we was w a t c h i n ?

SHE

Well
You was there.
You was there. He put you down and left.
Them scars you got is from when you tried to get the fire off me.

RACINE

I don't
re
mem
ber.

SHE

Ask your sister if she does.

(Anaia is looking away, trying to hide her face.)

RACINE

Twin?
Twin?
You cryin?

ANAIA

Umsicktomystomach.
Um sick.

(Anaia tries to run away.)

RACINE

Twin? Damn. All emotional.

SHE

Where you goin?

(Anaia stops in her tracks.)

Ya can't outrun it
Girl.
Iss gonna meet you wherever you go.

ANAIA

I
thought   I thought
                    you was dancin
                                        wigglin on the ground like that i thought it was a dance or somethin. I see it all the time I see it I see you dancin on the ground with the fire on you like a dress.

SHE

Shh. Quit cryin, baby. No need to cry.

RACINE

She's sorry, Mama. She just . . . you know.

SHE

Iss somethin I need y'all to do but I don't think y'all gon be able to do it if she's steady cryin.

RACINE

We can do it. We can. We're strong. Ain't we strong, 'Naia?

ANAIA

Yeah.

RACINE

We're strong. We can do anything.

SHE

Good.
I'ma keep this real simple:
Make your daddy dead
dead
dead
And everything around him you can destroy, too
I think he got some b i t c h

Kill his spirit, then the body
like he did me

Make him dead real dead

And bring me back some treasures from it.

Gotta do it quick, too. My body ready to go. We on a time crunch.

All the way **dead**.

(A silence.)

RACINE

Uh uh uh uh uh
uh uh uh uhhhh

RACINE AND ANAIA

Uh uh uhhhh uh uh uh
uh uh uh uh uh

RACINE

Mama
we respect that you dyin and all, but uhh
this seems a little
crazy—

SHE

Not as crazy as settin a woman on fire in front of her own kids then abandoning them to go off and start another life like nothin ever happened.

RACINE

. . .

Okay. You got a point. But uh uhmm
don't you think that since you dyin you might wanna just forgive and forget?

Die in a peaceful state?

SHE

Peace will come when he go.

RACINE

But Mama—

SHE

When he go

ANAIA

We ain't killers—

SHE

Anaia, pull this sheet offa me.

(Anaia does so. A moment during which the twins are aghast. Their mother's body is a hideous thing on the sheets.)

No peace 'til I know he gone.
You gonna do this for your mother? This one thing 'fore I die?

RACINE

We'll do it.

SHE

Good, good. Good girls. Dead. Real dead. And bring me back a piece.

ANAIA

I don't think—

RACINE

Just tell us how to find him.

SHE

I don't know where he at but The Lawyer is out in Californ-eye-ayy near the City of Angels. Chuck Hall—I'll never forget the name. Chuck. Hall. He in The Valley. He gon know where your daddy's at. Go find him and make him tell you.

He a slippery motherfucker, so be careful.

Dead, real dead. Lotsa blood is fine.

GOING WEST

The twins are traveling west throughout the following:

RACINE

Hey Twin.

ANAIA

Yeah.

RACINE

You ain't sick to your stomach no more?

ANAIA

No.

RACINE

Good. Well.   She is our mama.

ANAIA

But she ain't never came for us, never asked for us—

RACINE

I'm sure she kept track of where we was at—

ANAIA

It ain't the same.

RACINE

How was she gon come see us lookin like that?

ANAIA

Like what?

RACINE

Like scary. You know good and well you woulda shit yourself when you was twelve if she'da come see you lookin like that talkin 'bout

"I'm your long lost Mama."

ANAIA

I guess you right.

RACINE

Iss just one thing she want us to do before she die.

ANAIA

Yeah. But we ain't killers.

RACINE

I am.

ANAIA

No, you ain't. Who you done killed?

RACINE

Don't worry 'bout all that.

ANAIA

Damn, 'Cine. I mean. She our mama.

RACINE

Right.

ANAIA

And she made us, so she kinda like God, like you said—

RACINE

Eyup, eyup—

ANAIA

And he ain't even like us.

RACINE

Nope. So. So you ready?

ANAIA

. . . Eyup.

RACINE

Good. We gon do this. We gon do it right.

(They travel in silence for a bit.)

ANAIA

I favor Her.

RACINE

Who. God?

ANAIA

Eyup. The scars I got on my face she got on her whole self.

RACINE

Yeah.

ANAIA

I'm glad I favor somebody.

RACINE

Yeah. It do look like she spit you out.
Wonder who spit me out.

ANAIA

You prolly a combo between both of 'em.

RACINE

I 'on know. Whatchoo think he look like?

ANAIA

Like a skunk or a snake. Or a giant with a smelly beard. He prolly got a beer belly.

RACINE

How we gonna kill him?

ANAIA

I don't know.

RACINE

A gun?

ANAIA

Where we gon get a gun?

RACINE

Steal one or something.

ANAIA

That ain't no good plan. We should just poison him.

RACINE

With what?

ANAIA

Strychnine. Arsenic.

RACINE

That seem old-fashioned.

ANAIA

At least he'll be dead and we ain't gotta really get no blood on us. I don't like blood.

RACINE

But God said lotsa blood is okay.

ANAIA

Still.

RACINE

Poison is a punk ass bitch ass way to kill somebody. I think we should take a hammer to him.

ANAIA

You sick.

RACINE

I could do it. Be just like bustin open an egg.

ANAIA

Nasty.

RACINE

Or stab him?

ANAIA

Eugh. The sound of his body gettin stabbed like meat. I'ma be sick.

RACINE

I know! We'll push him off a building.

ANAIA

What building?

RACINE

We'll find one. We'll get him there close to the edge and push him.

ANAIA

What if he grab one of us on the way down?

RACINE

What if we knock him out
then throw him off the building?

ANAIA

How hard do you have to hit someone to knock them out? I don't like it.

RACINE

You don't like any of it.

ANAIA

I 'on know
I 'on know about this, 'Cine.
We ain't killers—

RACINE

How you figure that? We come from a man who tried to kill our mama and a mama who wants to kill that man. Iss in the blood.

ANAIA

I'ma be sick.   I bet he just look like an ordinary man.

I used to dream about a lady in a fire and I didn't know why.

THE WEAPON

The outskirts of the City of Angels. Racine picks up a sizable rock.

RACINE

Take your sock off.

(Anaia does so. Racine places the rock in the sock and ties a knot. Ha.)

ANAIA

That for what I think iss for?

RACINE

Eyup. Feels right. Like Cain and Abel or something.

ANAIA

She gon get her blood, I guess.

(They walk on.)

IN THE VALLEY

The twins stand before the door of a law office in The Valley.

RACINE

Just follow my lead.

(Racine knocks on the door. We're very suddenly inside the office. Hall sits at a desk.)

HALL

A Mister Chuck Wendell Hall sits at an immense desk in a North Hollywood office building. The desk was his grandfather's.
Pure oak very recently refurbished.
The kind of desk that makes a statement.
He sits behind the heavy desk, sweating. It is the dead of summer.
Sweating rivers and rivers.

He wears a shirt with a collar. Expensive. And a necktie, loosened. Also expensive.
If one were to look below the desk, one would see that he's wearing Bermuda shorts—not terribly expensive. Orange-ish.
No shoes or socks on his feet.

Dead of summer.

He belches. There is tequila warming in a glass somewhere nearby. A fat black fly perched on the edge of the glass contemplates a swim.
His hand shaking, he takes a bottle of pills from his Bermuda shorts pocket and attempts to unscrew the cap.
Nothing. Child lock. Fuck.
He tries again, pressing down. The cap opens and he pours the entire contents of the bottle onto the desk:

One, two, three . . .
placing the pills side by side—a pill parade:

four, five, six, seven . . .
He reaches for the glass of tequila and the fly buzzes angrily away. Gulp. It barely burns he's been drinking for hours.

eight, nine, tennn, eleven, twelf, thirteeeen . . .
He talks to the pills:

I'm going to follow you all straight
home
I'm going to follow you
home, take me there
fourteen, f if t ee n, s e v e n teen

it is hard to count, three hours he's been drinking

e i g h t e e n
n i n e t e e n

Okay, okay. Here we go!

And he swallows one—

(A knock at the door.)

I'm not here I'm out to lunch I'm retired go away.

(Another knock.)

I'm gone! Another pill.

(A loud bang. He goes to the door and opens it. The twins are standing there.)

Who
the
eff you?
are

RACINE

Are you Mr. Hall?

HALL

I'm not
here.

(Trying to slam the door in their faces, he stumbles and falls to the ground.)

Oh. Shit.

ANAIA

He's drunk.

RACINE

Are you Hall?

HALL

Why should I tell you anything? I work for—hiccup—
my own self!

ANAIA

I think this is him.

RACINE

That's his name on the door.

ANAIA

But he's drunk.

RACINE

What that mean?

ANAIA

We can't
if he's drunk we can't do it!

RACINE

Can't do what?

ANAIA

Rough him up or anything. It wouldn't be nice!

HALL

You're not the boss of me I'm the boss of myself!

RACINE

Shut up!

HALL

Don't you tell me to shut up! This is my place.
I built it from the ground up.
You can't just come into a person's place and tell them what to do.

RACINE

Definitely him.

HALL

Gaddamn right.

RACINE

Sit down.

HALL

I will. But not because you told me to. I'm sitting down because it's what I wanna do.

RACINE

Sure.

ANAIA

Stinks in here.

HALL

That's 'cause Luna's been shitting everywhere with no regard for anyone but herself.

RACINE

Who's Luna?

HALL

My receptionist. Just kidding. The cat. It was my receptionist's cat but she left it behind when she left me. Ha haha but your face, though.
You thought it was a human I was talkin about. Can you imagine some lady squatting in the corner to drop a deuce? Ha haHa.

ANAIA

You're disgusting.

HALL

I know that you think I don't know that. It's what she said all the time before she left.

(Imitating a female voice:)

> "Why don't you shave the back of your neck? You feel like a woolly mammoth. It's disgusting"

With so much hate. She said it with so much Like she couldn't stand the very ground I was walking on How'd that happen We had been in love it had been love I tell you the first time I saw her—

RACINE

Shut up!

ANAIA

Don't.

RACINE

We need to ask you some things, Mr. Hall.

HALL

Do I know you?

RACINE

Yes.

ANAIA

No.

RACINE

We might know some people in common.

HALL

Like who?

RACINE

A man from a long time ago. Tried to kill his wife. Ring a bell?

HALL

Lotta bells in the world Church bells, Wedding bells We didn't get married in a church We went right on down to the courthouse and got it done She wore a yellow sundress with—

RACINE

Sir, we need you to focus.

ANAIA

Yes. Please focus.

HALL

I am focused. I'm focused. Hell, I won Most Focused once. Irving Middle School Choir—

RACINE

O, my god—

HALL

I did! Don't talk to me about focus.

ANAIA

Alright, fine. Sir, we really need to find him soon. We on a time crunch. A man who tried to kill his wife eighteen years ago. He was a client of yours. Think about it.

HALL

Thinking, thinking. Mmmmmmmmmnope. Nothing. Don't know who that is.

RACINE

You're lyin.

HALL

Imagine that.

(Racine raises the rock-sock.)

What's that for?

(She holds it up higher.)

ANAIA

'Cine.

RACINE

I'm gonna have to pop your fat head if you don't quit playin.

HALL

With that?

RACINE

What else?

(Hall is laughing really hard.)

HALL

Is that a rock in there?
You're gonna hit me to death with
a sock?

(Racine swings the rock. He dodges.)

ANAIA

'Cine! Don't—

HALL

Missed me!

(Racine swings again, again Hall dodges.)

ANAIA

Just give him a chance to tell us—

(Racine swings and Hall dodges. He laughs to beat the band.)

HALL

Okay. No. But seriously. I'm already on my way out. You almost missed me.

L o o k i t here.

(Holds up the pill bottle and laughs some more.)

ANAIA

What's that?

HALL

Pills!
to dispatch myselffff

Soft and hard and soft
I t o o k 'em I t o o k 'em I t o o k 'em So Glory is coming!
You're too late!
I am bathed in Glory—

RACINE

What's he talking about?

HALL

You see these shorts? Glory.
Got them in Bermuda.
Lotsa people have Bermuda shorts they didn't actually get in Bermuda—

ANAIA

I think he's sayin he done already took some pills to kill himself so he don't care about that rock.

HALL

That is precisely what he's saying. I've already taken a few of these. One is enough to do the magic. Two is enough to have me dance my way to hell. What do you think I'll get for a few? I dunno, is it five by now?

(Hall swallows a few more pills. Racine lowers the rock.)

ANAIA

He ain't gonna tell us nothin. He ain't scared to die. Guess we gotta go.

RACINE

We ain't done with this fool. We gotta find out where—

ANAIA

C'mon, 'Cine . . .

RACINE

We got to!

ANAIA

Let's just look around. He's got files and things—

RACINE

It'll take forever to go through all these files! God's finna die!

(Notices that Hall is nodding off.)

Shit. He's falling asleep—
Hey. Hey. You can't fall asleep yet.

HALL

Why   not?

(Nodding off.)

ANAIA

Please stay awake! God's finna die and we gotta find out where he at so we can go see him before She do.

HALL

The man you're looking for is your dad.

ANAIA

Sort of. He fathered us.

HALL

Tall man. Dark man. Lit a lady on fire about twenty years ago.

RACINE

Yeah, that's the one!

HALL

He lied about it real g o o d
could
tell he was lying
but I honestly
wassso scared of him, I just pretended.

RACINE

What happened?

HALL

In court he said she lit herself on fire
and we presented old suicide notes she wrote when they broke up
Bastard had them in his pocket when he came to see me, before they could even arrest him.
R e a l c a l m and c o o l. Knew he would get off.

RACINE

Where he go after y'all won the court case?

HALL

Up into the hills.

ANAIA

Beverly Hills?

HALL

Castaic. Just up the 5.
Little yellow house on the highest hill.
Teal shutters.

Went there for dinner once.
Didn't want to. But.
Neat house. Dog and everything. You'd never know.

RACINE

He livin in a yellow house?

ANAIA

With a dog?

HALL

Last
I saw
him.

ANAIA

What he look like?

HALL

Like like
he ate
all
the
canaries and . . .

(Hall falls asleep. Anaia shakes him.)

ANAIA

Mister? Mister?

(Hall is very suddenly awake again.)

HALL

And he must have a special kind of jizz

'cause he had more
two others boys
twinzzzz

ANAIA

Twins?
He got another set of twins?

HALL

All the c a n a r i e s.

(And he succumbs to the pills. They stare at his body a moment.)

RACINE

God said to bring treasure. Iss treasure here.

(She raises the rock and hits the body. Anaia runs away. The lights dim. Sound of rock hitting flesh and Anaia retching.)

UP TO THE HILLS

Racine and Anaia are climbing a steep hill.

RACINE

Twin?
Why you slowin down?

ANAIA

Just got a buzzin in my side.

RACINE

You wanna take a rest? We shouldn't be walking all this way anyhow. Iss far. Maybe we can thumb a ride or somethin.

(Anaia sits in the dust.)

Sun's going down. We can just sleep out here. It'll be like camping.

ANAIA

'Cept we finna go kill somebody.

(Anaia sings softly to herself.)

RACINE

We been killt.

ANAIA

Whatchoo mean? We breathin.

RACINE

But what we breathin if it ain't been nobody around to tell us we got mouths and lungs and that make us people like everybody else, you know?

ANAIA

Naw, I don't.

RACINE

I mean we floatin.
We land from time to time and get stepped on but thas it.
Ain't been nobody around to give us some
I don't know
some foundation?
No real mama. No real daddy. Nobody.

ANAIA

You so mad.

RACINE

Ain't you? I wanna step on somethin for once. See what it feel like. Must feel good.
You 'member Second Foster Daddy?

ANAIA

Mmm hmm. With his fat ass.

RACINE

'Member how he used to snap the belt at us?

ANAIA

Wasn't no "us," that was you. 'Cause you laughed every time he came down the stairs, so you always got a whuppin.

RACINE

Eyup, eyup.

ANAIA

And you used to call for Her. For God. I'd hear you callin for Her from the next room when he was hitting you—

RACINE

For Mama?

ANAIA

Eyup. You'd be cryin out for Her.

RACINE

Thas a lie.

ANAIA

No it ain't. I heard you. Ear against the wall—

RACINE

You ain't heard me cry. I never cried one time when he was hittin me. Thas why he wouldn't stop. Fat motherfucking fat bitch ass motherfucker. He the first person I killt.

ANAIA

You ain't killed him. He had a heart attack.

RACINE

He had it 'cause he kept whuppin me.
He kept whuppin me 'cause I kept doin stuff to make him whup me
'cause I knew it would kill his fat ass.
Fat fuckin ass.

ANAIA

Damn.

RACINE

Yeah.

ANAIA

Twin?

RACINE

Yeah?

ANAIA

Damn.

RACINE

I know.

ANAIA

You in a room gettin whupped, God layin up with alligator skin, we got these scars and h e i n a y e l l o w h o u s e with t e a l s h u t t e r s

and a dog and t w i n s?

RACINE

Eyup.

ANAIA

New pair. Fresh pair uh twins.

RACINE

Don't I know it.
I know it. I know.

ANAIA

I like my ugly.

RACINE

You ain't ugly.

ANAIA

I am and I like it.

RACINE

Stop that.

ANAIA

For real. It keeps me safe. Ain't gotta talk to as many stupid people. They just stay outta my way. Don't nobody ever hand me no flyer on a street corner. Iss like a super power.
Damn. I'm burnin.

RACINE

Me, too. Scar be burnin like iss still some fire in there tryna come out.
You ever wanna scrape your scars off and see what's underneath?

ANAIA

Wouldn't nothin be underneath but dead.

RACINE

Might be somethin else under there.
I dunno. You might look. Different. You ever wonder?

ANAIA

No point. What we gonna do about them other twins, Twin?

RACINE

God said to destroy everything around him—

ANAIA

She said we could. She said we could destroy everything around him.

RACINE

Well.

ANAIA

"Well" what?
They innocent. They can't help bein his kids.

RACINE

Ain't nobody innocent.
They prolly sit up at dinner and laugh about us and God.

ANAIA

No, they don't, 'Cine. Stop that.

RACINE

Sheeid.

ANAIA

They ain't done nothin to us. C'mon now.

RACINE

Fine. Fine. Fine.

(Anaia sings a bit to herself.)

ANAIA

Wish it was some ice out here, Twin.

RACINE

Me, too.

THE HOUSE ON THE HILL

A modest house in the sleepy desert city of Castaic, CA. Sound of the family dog barking. Riley, Scotch and Angie are home.

RILEY

The eldest brother by two minutes, Riley, is watering the succulents on the balcony.

SCOTCH

The younger brother, Scotch, yes, after the liquor, is in his bedroom writing the best fucking poetry you've ever heard. If anyone asks, he'll say it's for school but really it's for him. Them words.

ANGIE

Their mother, Angela, is in the driveway unloading the car of a week's worth of groceries.

You boys eat like freaking cows! The least you could do is come and help me unload.

RILEY

Coming.

SCOTCH

Coming.

ANGIE

Neither is actually coming. Angie stands in the driveway, the trunk of her car open. Two cartons of eggs, blueberries, frozen waffles—mostly for them.
Sweat on her neck she will NOT be carrying these bags in herself
It's bad enough she had to go to the store and make sure make sure make sure
she got the right brand of bacon and the correct level of milk fat
It's bad enough the clerk wouldn't accept the coupon for the peanut butter.
Expired. Expired? Expired.
It's bad enough she stepped in gum and it won't come off the bottom of her shoe no matter what she does it won't come off—come off! It won't
Come and get these bags I won't bring them in.
She won't, either. They can sit in this driveway and melt and churn and spoil
She won't do it
I'll leave them here!
She will too but not really. She'd hate for all of this stuff to go to waste and the time it took to get them and anyway, she'd end up looking crazy to the neighbors who were probably already looking, peeking up the hill at the house
The top of this hill feels like being in a fishbowl
Riley? Scotch?

RILEY AND SCOTCH

Coming.

RILEY

Riley's all about the succulents. They don't really need much water but it's an excuse
She's embarrassing, down there yelling and dowdy with all of her groceries.
So effing house-wife-y, it's embarrassing. So why not water the succulents or pretend to? Hey, bruh. You should go help Mom.

SCOTCH

Scotch's poetry is so dope that he refuses to stop writing.
I mean, the piece uses barbecue as a metaphor for love
Barbecue as a metaphor for love—chyeah!
Brilliance   I can't, bruh. I'm writing!

RILEY

He can't effng write.

ANGIE

Her bunion hurts. She has a bunion. God.

RILEY

His metaphors are always clunky.

ANGIE

There are blackbirds circling above. Maybe they know about the bunion.
Dead of summer.

RILEY

Mom, Scotch is gonna come help you.

SCOTCH

Scotch recites:
"And, girl, if the sauce gets too dry
on our road to love, girl
If the sauce gets too dry
from the length of time spent
on the hot coals of life . . ."
This shit so dope!

ANGIE

Angie hates her life.

The man occasionally walks into a room and gives her a look like He wishes she'd disappear already. The kids won't let her touch them
And the bunion. Frig. She can't cuss. Hasn't had a good cuss since the kids.
Your father will be home soon and when He sees these groceries out here He's going to be very angry!
. . .

RILEY, SCOTCH AND ANGIE

Who's she kidding?

ANGIE

Tired and pissed does not equal fool.
She will put the groceries away.
The man is not the sort . . .

She will put the groceries away. Frig.

RILEY

Go help Mom.

SCOTCH

Shit so dope!

RILEY

Dang.

(He looks over the railing of the balcony.)

Her mom jeans are extra mom-ish today. Sucks teeth.
I got it, Mom. I got it.

RACINE

A few yards away hiding behind a neighbor's minivan.

ANAIA

She's pretty.

RACINE

So?

ANAIA

Just sayin she's pretty.

RACINE

Don't.

RILEY

(Carrying groceries) You got everything, huh?

ANGIE

What took you so long to come help me?

RILEY

Sorry. Was watering the plants.

(Riley and Angie make their way inside.)

ANGIE

Has your father called?

RILEY

Nope.

ANGIE

Probably working late tonight.

SCOTCH

What's for dinner?

ANGIE

You can eat anything you helped me carry inside.

SCOTCH

Aw, man, Mom, don't be mad. I'm writing.

ANGIE

Angie refuses to be another tired, middle-aged woman. She refuses. Going out tonight.

SCOTCH

Yeah. Clayton and I were thinking of hitting up a spot—

ANGIE

No. I'm going out tonight. Me.

RILEY

You?

(The twins look at their mother.)

SCOTCH

With Dad?

ANGIE

With Mrs. Orson.

SCOTCH

What, y'all goin to a tea party or something? Ha haha

ANGIE

That's really funny. No. It's a party. Just a regular one.

SCOTCH

You gonna make dinner before you go?

RILEY

Don't listen to him, Mom.

ANGIE

I'm not.

(Angie goes upstairs.)

RILEY

Such a spoiled brat.

SCOTCH

What? Y'all need to stop oppressing me for being so committed to my writing process. I'm trying to make us all rich.

RILEY

Yeah, yeah.

SCOTCH

What are you making for dinner?

RILEY

Probably do an arugula salad. It's coniferous. Detoxifying.

SCOTCH

Are you tryna be wack or does that happen by accident? I'm just askin.

ANGIE

Upstairs in the master bedroom, the eyeliner pencil is slippery.
It is the dead of summer and the boys don't know what she's planning.
No one knows, not even Mrs. Orson, about the suitcase packed in the trunk ready to take her to Yucca Valley where she'll hide out with a friend and then take the bus to Vegas where she'll gamble no less than three hundred of the seven grand she's been saving before taking the train up to Connecticut, where a new name and job are waiting for her.
He doesn't hit, He's never done that.

but

but

That look He gave her when she asked
about what happened with His ex-wife
That look was. Hm.

That look   that look was   that was a l o o k that hmmm

(Riley knocks on the door.)

RILEY

Mom?

ANGIE

What is it, Riley? I'm getting dressed.

RILEY

Do you want some salad for the road? Arugula?

ANGIE

Had this come from her body?
No, Son. I'm fine. I'll eat out.

RILEY

Okay.

Mom?

ANGIE

Son?

RILEY

i love you.

ANGIE

Had this come from her body? I know, Son.

(Angie opens the door to the room and touches Riley's face.)

I love you, too.

(Angie makes her way down the stairs and out the front door.)

Tell your father I'll be back later on. Keep the door closed. We aren't cooling the neighborhood. Scotch—clean your ears. They're dripping. God. Don't you feel that?

SCOTCH

All of my feeling goes into my work.

ANGIE

Take care.

SCOTCH AND RILEY

Bye, Mom.

(As soon as she closes the door, Scotch turns up the radio. It is incredibly loud. Riley puts in headphones and makes dinner. Scotch may thrash to his music.

Angie steps outside and closes the front door. She gives the house a good, long look and then the finger. She gets into the car and drives a bit but doesn't get very far. The twins are sitting in the middle of the road. Anaia sings softly to herself, looking away. Racine stares directly at Angie.)

IN THE ROAD

ANGIE

Hello? Hello? Excuse me?
Uh.   Hi? Can you hear me? Helllllloooooooooo!

RACINE

We just gon ask her where he at. Thas it. Thas it, 'Naia. You shakin. Stop.

ANGIE

HELLOOOOO

ANAIA

Ain't you gonna say somethin?

RACINE

She gotta come to us.

ANGIE

Girls? Can you move, please? Shoo. Shoo!

RACINE

Who this bitch think she shooin?

(Angie takes the keys out of the ignition, climbs out of the car, walking toward the twins.)

ANGIE

Excuse me, but I've got to be somewhere and
are you two okay? Is everything alright?

RACINE

We fine.

ANGIE

She doesn't look well.

RACINE

She's fine. You know us?

ANGIE

Know you? Uh. No. Should I?

RACINE

We're his first ones.

ANGIE

Who?

ANAIA

His first kids. We're the ones he had first.

ANGIE

O. O.
You're alive?

RACINE

Naw, we're zombies.

ANGIE

He said
He said
you died in some kind of fire and He didn't have to pay child support.
Are you here for child support?

(She takes off her pearl necklace, coming closer.)

Real. Japanese Akoya.

RACINE

Don't nobody want your pearls.

ANGIE

Well, this what I've got to offer.

RACINE

You got more to offer.

ANGIE

I need the car.

RACINE

You ain't in no position to be tellin us what you need.
You know what our mama's been doin while you been layin up in your big yellow house with them teal shutters?

ANAIA

Our mama been up in a bed wastin away. He burnt up most of her body. She a crisp.

RACINE

Eyup. He tried to kill Her.
And us, too. See? Fire bit me on my back and arms and 'Naia on her face.

ANGIE

I'm so sorry. That is unfortunate. But I hope you understand
that that He lied to me—

RACINE

You knew he was lyin.

ANAIA

'Cine—

ANGIE

I didn't.

RACINE

Yeah, you did.

ANGIE

I did not.

RACINE

'Naia, who this heffa think she foolin? Can't even lie straight.

ANAIA

I don't know, 'Cine. She could be tellin the truth—

RACINE

You was sittin up in a yellow house with teal shutters while Daddy number three was makin us wash his drawz and make him macaroni outa box and lickin his lips anytime I came in the room with my shoulders showin—

ANAIA

Let's just let her go—

RACINE

You was sittin up in a blood house, a house he got to put a mask on what he done to us. You ain't ask no questions?

(Angie tries to walk back to the car but Racine blocks her path.)

ANGIE

Please. I've got to get away.

RACINE

We couldn't get away. Ain't never worn no pearls. You, 'Naia?

ANAIA

Never even held none.

RACINE

I like that car. It's a fair reward for all we been through, I think.

ANGIE

It's mine.

RACINE

Iss ours. He never gave us nothin.
He gave you a lot. And somma what he gave you shoulda been ours.

ANGIE

I'm sorry that He—

RACINE

Gimme them keys.

ANGIE

No.

RACINE

What ? Is you stupid?

(Racine tries to grab the keys from Angie, but Angie resists. They struggle a bit.)

Gimme the keys, bitch! Give 'em to me!

ANGIE

They're mine!

(Racine manages to wrench the keys from Angie's hand. She holds them up, gleefully.)

RACINE

Got 'em.

ANGIE

They don't belong to you!

RACINE

Thas whatchyo mouth say!
Look at her, 'Naia. She ain't used to not getting what she wants.

ANGIE

That's just
That's just mean.

RACINE

"That's just
That's just mean." Ha ha ha HA ha!

ANGIE

You . . .you pair of animals. You're going to come and steal from me because of something He did?

ANAIA

We ain't animals. We on a mission. From God.

ANGIE

God?

RACINE

God is our mama.

ANGIE

O, that's right. Your "mama."

RACINE

I don't like the way you sayin "Mama" like that.

ANGIE

Well, I don't like having my property stolen by a couple of thieves!

ANAIA

We ain't thieves.

ANGIE

Yes you ARE! I just wanna get away
I just wanna
I've earned it
I planned for months
IF He comes home and
I tell Him the car's been stolen do you know
do you know what He'll . . .
goddamnit Angie you really thought you'd get away, didn't you you really thought you really did—

RACINE

Our mama ain't never had a shot like the one you got. Sheeid. You ain't special.

ANGIE

. . . It's not my fault
your weak, ghetto trashy "mama" got burned up! She should've left Him!

ANAIA, RACINE AND ANGIE

. . . .

ANAIA

. . . . uh . . . . umm

RACINE

uh huh, uh umm

ANAIA AND RACINE

uh um ummm

ANAIA

. . . . Bitch . . .

RACINE

. . . hold up hold up holdup . . . this Bitch,

ANAIA

"Weak"?
"Ghetto trashy"?

RACINE

Bitch, where you get all that from?

ANAIA

This bitch done called God "ghetto trashy"!

ANGIE

Each of us is responsible for how our lives turn out! If you were educated, you'd understand that—

(Racine hits Angie in the face with the rock.)

RACINE

We educated.

ANGIE

. . . you hit me . . .

ANAIA

Twin, don't—

RACINE

We educated, Bitch! Say it. Say we educated!

ANGIE

animal

(Racine hits Angie again.)

ANAIA

Racine!

ANGIE

. . . ow . . . h a r d—

(Racine hits Angie a few times. Anaia hides her face.)

a   i
        r.

(Angie is dead. Anaia whimpers.)

RACINE

Twin.

ANAIA

Yeah?

RACINE

You gonna be sick?

ANAIA

I don't   think   so.

RACINE

You want them pearls?

ANAIA

I 'Cine she dead?

RACINE

You ain't did nothin', so you cool. Iss all on me. If it come up, we'll just tell the truth. You want them pearls?

ANAIA

God might.

RACINE

God don't want nothin but blood.
Let's keep one of her nails. They nice. Manicured.

TWINS AND TWINS

Inside the house. Scotch and Riley are seated for a dinner of arugula, piled impossibly high.

SCOTCH

I hate you. You're the worst person alive.

RILEY

There's plenty of other food.

SCOTCH

Where do you think she really went?

RILEY

Don't know. Mexico?

SCOTCH

Dad's gonna find her.

RILEY

Yeah.

SCOTCH

Wanna hear a poem I wrote for her?

RILEY

No. Really, no.

SCOTCH

It's short.

RILEY

God. Please. No.

SCOTCH

It's an acrostic that doesn't announce itself:
Matriarch resistant to the matronly
Otherworldly, kind and compassionate
Thoughtful in times of woe or triumph
Holds heaven and earth in her hallowed hands
Even when nothing is enough,
Ride or die wit' it, never shy wit' it
Mother.

RILEY

I'm dead.

SCOTCH

Jealous.

(A knock at the door.)

RILEY

Get it. I ordered pizza.

(Scotch goes to the door and opens it. Anaia and Racine stand before him.)

SCOTCH

I know you?

RACINE

No.

ANAIA

Kind of.

RILEY

Who is it?

SCOTCH

Not pizza. Wait. Wait. Our birthday isn't for a couple of weeks but . . .

(Riley comes to the door.)

RILEY

I didn't actually order pizza . . .Who's this?

RACINE

I'm Racine.

ANAIA

Anaia.

RILEY, SCOTCH, ANAIA AND RACINE

Twins.

. . . .

SCOTCH

O shit.

O shit

O shit!

RILEY

What?

SCOTCH

Dad did this, I think.

RACINE

He definitely did.

SCOTCH

Come on in, girls! You can change upstairs. O shit O shit!

RILEY

Wait—what are you doing?

SCOTCH

Dad hired them!

RILEY

How do we know that?

SCOTCH

Look at them, Riley! Twins! Stripper twins!

RILEY

They don't look like—

SCOTCH

I should call Michael and Tyrell—

RACINE

Don't call anyone else. Private show.

SCOTCH

Okay. Whatever you say, cutie. Go on up. Second door on the left.

(Anaia and Racine head upstairs.)

Oh my god. Stripper Twins! Dad's a genius!

RILEY

This just doesn't seem like something he'd do.
Let me just call him and make sure he really sent them.

SCOTCH

(Imitating Riley) "Let me just call him . . ." Do you wake up in the morning and stroke your chin thinking of ways to be the lamest motherfucker ever? Damn.

RILEY

I just—

SCOTCH

It's our birthday.

RILEY

In two weeks.

SCOTCH

He always surprises us. Remember the turtles?

RILEY

Yes. In our beds while we slept—

SCOTCH

Twin fucking turtles we woke up to on our tenth birthday like it was muhfuckin Christmas!

RILEY

They stank.

SCOTCH

Muhfuckin Turtle Christmas!

RILEY

Kinda creepy if you ask me.

SCOTCH

Get excited with me, bro! Twins! We're about to get a striptease from a pair of TWINS! I gotta go get fresh. I call the pretty one. Ay ay ay! Twins!

(Scotch turns up the radio.)

DRESSING

Anaia and Racine get dressed in the sexiest clothes they can find in Angie's closet.

ANAIA

I don't like this I don't like this I don't like this

(Racine holds Anaia by her shoulders.)

RACINE

We almost there, 'Naia. People always quit just when they 'bout to reach the finish line. Now's not the time to be gettin all emotional. Come on. We almost there. He'll be home soon.

ANAIA

This ain't right.

RACINE

I said we're almost t h e r e ! Don't get all weak on me, now.

ANAIA

Fine, then! Go ahead and do what you wanna do but I don't want no part of it.

(Anaia turns to leave.)

RACINE

You don't want no part of it?
You is part of it!

(Anaia continues out the door.)

You just a lil punk!

ANAIA

I ain't no punk! Just ain't all hardened like you!

RACINE

"Hardened"? The fuck that mean?

ANAIA

Means you ain't got no soul or compassion!

RACINE

I got soul and compassion for GOD! Who's finna die!

ANAIA

But you ain't got none for nobody else.

RACINE

"But you ain't got none for nobody else." No, I don't!
And why should I?
Huh? Who you see around this motherfucker I should be havin soul and compassion for, huh?

ANAIA

Okay, fine, fine, fine. Shit. But you gotta promise me it ain't no more blood but his.

RACINE

I promise.

ANAIA

You gotta swear to God.

RACINE

Fine. I swear 'fore God and to God and I put that on everything. No more blood but his.

ANAIA

If you go back on it, I'm just gon walk away, Twin. Naw, I'm not gon walk. I'ma run.
You on your own.

RACINE

Let's just get ready.

ANAIA

I will.
Don't see why we gotta tease them like we strippers, tho.
Seem weird. They're our brothers—

RACINE

Don't you even say that or it becomes true.
They ain't nothin to us and we ain't nothin to them.
We on a mission. From God.

ANAIA

Twin?

RACINE

Yeah.

ANAIA

How you felt about killin that lady?

RACINE

I ain't felt no kinda way.
Don't look at me like that. I didn't feel nothin. She wasn't a nice lady. And she kinda stole from us. I don't feel nothin for her. All my feelings is for God.

ANAIA

Forreal?

RACINE

Eyup. God. In between them sheets with Her skin flakin off. God prolly ain't been touched by a man since he did it.

ANAIA

Nope.

RACINE

And what she say? "Ghetto trashy"?

ANAIA

I believe thas what she said.

RACINE

Now errbody know talkin shit about God will get you kilt.

ANAIA

Eyup.

RACINE

Struck down.

ANAIA

Right.

RACINE

We ain't nothin' but the hand of God doin Her bidding.

ANAIA

Right. You right.

THE TEASE

Anaia and Racine come down the stairs, dressed to strip. The radio plays stripping music. Riley is nearby, watching but not participating.

SCOTCH

Alright ladies! Let's see what you got!

(The women dance. Racine is much more free with her movement than Anaia. Racine gives Scotch a full on lap dance.)

Awww, yeahhh! Yes. Yeah, girl. Work that ass. Work. Hell yeah!

Riley! Twins, Riley! Twins! Hey you!

(Points to Anaia.)

I want you behind me. Put those titties on my neck.

(Anaia goes near to him, awkwardly dancing.)

Wait, wait, wait. Get behind me. Behind. I want this one in the front.

Riley? You better get in on this, bro. He did it for both of us.

RILEY

I'm alright.

SCOTCH

No you're not. You. Go dance with my brother.

(He's pointing at Anaia, who looks at Riley.)

RILEY

No, she doesn't need to do that. That's all you, Scotch.

SCOTCH

No, bruh. That's all *you*. I got the pretty one. That one's yours.

(Anaia isn't sure where to go. She and Racine look at one another. Anaia exits the house.)

Where's she goin? This isn't over yet. How long did he pay for? Riley?

RACINE

My sister ain't ugly.

SCOTCH

No, no. I guess, all God's children are beautiful, or whatever. Sure.

ALL FALL DOWN

Outside. Riley follows Anaia.

RILEY

Hey. Sorry I don't. I just don't think.
It's not because of your face or anything. I'm just. This is more Scotch's thing.
You want some water or something?

ANAIA

No.

RILEY

Okay. Want a coat? Someone might drive by and. Never mind.
So, how long did he pay for?

ANAIA

Who?

RILEY

My dad.

ANAIA

He didn't.

RILEY

He didn't?

ANAIA

No.

RILEY

I knew it. I knew you weren't strippers. You just don't have the—Something just didn't add up. So, what are you really?

ANAIA

Sick. I'ma little sick to my stomach.

RILEY

O. Anything I can do for you? You want something to eat? We've got arugula.

ANAIA

Thas alright.

RILEY

You sound like you're from somewhere in the South.

ANAIA

Eyup.

RILEY

My dad is, too.

ANAIA

. . . He ever talk about it?

RILEY

Not a lot. When he does it's usually to say something about how fucked up everyone down there is. How they enjoy swimming in their own misery.

ANAIA

Hm.

RILEY

I've never really been to the South. Well, Texas once. Austin. Band trip.

ANAIA

How old are you?

RILEY

We'll be seventeen in thirteen days.

ANAIA

Oh. Bet you got you a girlfriend.

RILEY

No.

ANAIA

Cute little kid like you?

RILEY

There's
there's this guy I like.

ANAIA

Oh. My bad.

RILEY

I hope you don't mind my asking . . . . . .What happened to your face?

ANAIA

Thas a secret.

(A scream from within the house.)

RILEY

You hear that?

ANAIA

Yeah. Seems like they're havin a good time.

(Another scream.)

RILEY

No No
That sounded bad.

ANAIA

They're fine. My sister, she just gets a little wild.

RILEY

Maybe I should—

ANAIA

It was a fire. Someone set a fire and it crawled onto my face and left me like this.

RILEY

O, wow. That sucks. Why would anyone do something like that?

ANAIA

Thas what I keep askin myself. How could he?

RILEY

He? You know who did it?

(Another scream as Scotch runs out of the house.)

SCOTCH

R i l e y ! !

I don't

I I don't think they're
strippers—

(Scotch falls to the ground, crawling. We can see a knife stuck in his back.)

RILEY

Scotch! Scotch! There's a knife in you!

SCOTCH

Is that
w h a t t h a t i
s?

(Riley tries to pull the knife from his brother's back.)

No
hurts
no

RILEY

O
my god O my god
what
O my god
How O my god

(Racine appears from inside the house, less dressed than when we last saw her, and bloody. She holds the sock. Riley tries to stop the blood pouring out of his brother with his hands.)

SCOTCH

I
i i i'm—

RILEY

Don't.
DON'T!

SCOTCH

ahh h ha ha l a m e . . .

(Scotch is gone.)

RILEY

Ha ha HA ha haHa ha
ha haha ha hahhaha
HAHA Ha hah haha

Scotch is
Scotch is
Scotch is my
twin dead!

Scotch is my twin is
Ha aha hAHAhaha haha Ha HaaaaaAAA
He's dead His blood is He's gone
My twin
Gone

This is f u nn y y y y

ha ha HAHA ha hahA Ha ha a h a ha h aaaa ha
HHhhaa

Ha ha HAA HA HA HA ha hahaha
ha ahhah he's bleeeeding arugula
arugula on his SHIRT ha ha ha! Ha
And and and and and he HATES arugula! Ha ha ha!

RACINE

Look like he done went crazy.

ANAIA

Yeah. Yeah.

RACINE

He called you ugly. I didn't plan to do it, but he called you ugly.

ANAIA

I am, though.

RACINE

If we don't do the other one, he's gonna tell.

ANAIA

What? No.

RACINE

You don't have to watch. You can go inside.

ANAIA

You said . . .you said . . .

RACINE

He'll talk. He might even blame you even though you didn't do it—

ANAIA

We talked. Me and him.

RACINE

What that mean?

ANAIA

Means we can't.

(Racine goes to approach Riley but Anaia stands in her way.)

RACINE

You in my way.

ANAIA

You keep doin it. You said we'd just do him and not them but—

RACINE

I'm doin what's best for us—

ANAIA

You a lie.

RACINE

Get the fuck outta my way, Twin—

(Racine tries to pass Anaia, but Anaia shoves her.)

G i r r r l

(Anaia shoves her sister again.)

Punk ass.
Punk ass bitch!
Say it. Say "I'm a punk ass weak ass bitch"—

ANAIA

Stop.

RACINE

If you start cryin, I swear to God—

ANAIA

Twin—

RACINE

You in my way. God gon be mad when I tell Her—

RILEY

Why are you doing this?

ANAIA

Because your daddy is our daddy and he—

RACINE

Don't talk to him!

RILEY

My dad is . . .?

ANAIA

Your dad did a bad thing to our mama.

RACINE

Jesus Christ.

RILEY

O. That sucks.

RACINE

Let's do him before he gets away and tells on us—

RILEY

Is He the one that burned you?

ANAIA

Yes. And I know it's not your fault. Don't worry. We're not going to hurt you.

RACINE

This shit right here

(Anaia sits beside Riley.)

RILEY

Thank you.

(Riley grabs Anaia's throat. Racine hits Riley with the sock. He collapses.)

RACINE

What I tell you? Huh? You wanna make conversation with him? You so—

(Riley has gotten up and tackles Racine. He bests her and straddles her body, his fingers tight around her neck. Anaia tries unsuccessfully to get him off her sister.)

RILEY

Crazy crazy bitch! You want to come to my house and kill my brother Bitch I don't care what He did Die! Die, you. Die There you go. Just go. Die. Stupid, filthy, disgusting, dog bitch Die die die Die die—

(Anaia has hit Riley as hard as she can on the back of his head with the sock. She hits him again and again until he gurgles, twitches, and is still. Anaia goes to Racine, shaking her.)

ANAIA

O—'Cine—he's gone—I—I did it—he's—

. . .

Twin? Twin? 'Cine, get up.

(Sound of a car approaching. She looks in the direction it's coming from—up the driveway. She shakes Racine again.)

Get up. Somebody's comin.

(The car stops. Anaia lifts her sister, dragging her out of view. She waits. A car door opens and closes and Man gets out. We hear hard-soled shoes on the ground. He stops near Riley's body for a moment. He continues, stopping at Scotch's body. He walks near the bushes, very close to where Anaia is hiding, then turns again toward the car.

In the driveway he takes off his shoes and socks, slowly, methodically. He removes his suit jacket and tie. He rolls up his pant's legs, whistling. Finally, he takes off his hat, and we see his face for the first time.)

MAN

This slope continues right on up just behind the house. Pretty easy climb if you're in decent shape.
Meet me at the top.

Or. You could just stay in those bushes
and wonder.

(Man climbs the aforementioned hill. Anaia emerges from the bushes, laying her sister down on the ground carefully.)

ANAIA

Twin. He's here. I'm gonna . . .
I got the sock. I got it.

(She follows Man up the hill.)

SHOWDOWN

Anaia and Man stand on opposite sides of the hill.

MAN

You still kinda pretty. Kinda. You ain't a complete monster. I was worried.

ANAIA

Huhwhat?

MAN

Well, maybe just plain "pretty" in general is a stretch. You're prettier than I left her, that's for sure. Well. You want to ask me some questions, I imagine.

ANAIA

Huhwhat?

MAN

How about if I ask one and then you ask one. You first.

ANAIA

I I

I don't know—

MAN

Yes, you do.

ANAIA

I
Why did you set her on fire?

MAN

Because she wouldn't let me hold her.

ANAIA

You set—wait, what does that—

MAN

My turn. Who'd you kill first?

ANAIA

I didn't kill nobody. Not really, 'cept in self defense. 'Cine was the one—

MAN

Who first?

ANAIA

Your wife.

MAN

Angie?

ANAIA

Thas her name? Yeah.

MAN

Wow.

ANAIA

My turn. What does that mean "she wouldn't let me hold her"? Huh? You were mad 'cause she didn't want you to touch her so you set her on fire?

MAN

It's more nuanced than that, but yes.

ANAIA

That don't strike you as a bit of an overreaction?

MAN

My turn. How'd she die?

ANAIA

Your wife? Rock in a sock. You don't think you overreacted a lil bit?

MAN

It was an appropriate response by a man out of control, I admit. I was young.

ANAIA

"Appropriate"? "Appropriate"? You are really sick.

MAN

You ever have a blemish you want to get rid of very, very badly? A blackhead, maybe? You ever squeeze the blackhead until it falls off but there's pus underneath still hanging around? Reminding you of the ugliness of that blackhead? Then it becomes about getting rid of the pus with peroxide or whatever you can find that'll sting just a little so you know it's working? You ever just need to put a thing out because it has been so catastrophic to your very being?

ANAIA

Pus?

MAN

I was young.

ANAIA

Just something for you to get rid of?

MAN

I was young. And I'm sorry. Next thing I did was go down to the bridge over the river and hang over it, ready to jump in so I could join you all in death.

ANAIA

But you didn't.

MAN

No. And thankfully, you all survived.

ANAIA

But you went to court and got off and God is in a bed burnt to a crisp and I'm so ugly no one'll look me in my e y e s.

MAN

I'm sorry about that. But it isn't just my fault. You've got to factor in every piece of the puzzle.

ANAIA

Every p i e c e of the
p u z z l e ?
What other pieces are there?

MAN

She could've let me hold her. She could've opened herself up to me. She could've let me fully stand up in my house. I needed that as a young man. Just to fully stand.
I don't expect you to understand.

ANAIA

Igotababycomin.
You're the granddad.
A baby.

MAN

You're not a killer.

ANAIA

What am I gonna tell the baby 'bout all of this?

MAN

Put that thing down. You can tell it you made a few mistakes when you were young. Like I did.

ANAIA

How am I gonna tell it 'bout God and 'Cine and you?

'Bout how you tried to
k i l l us all.

MAN

"Kill us all"?
I didn't try to kill you all. Just her. You think I set my own babies on fire? She did that. She screamed and grabbed ahold of you two.
I couldn't get her to let go. That's when I ran out.
That's why I stood on that bridge and nearly let myself fall in.
You think I tried to kill my own babies? Is that what she told you?

ANAIA

. . .

MAN

I didn't. She lied.

ANAIA

I promised God I'd bring back a piece of you.

MAN

I'm telling you, she lied. You've got to give this up.
Otherwise it's just going to be bad for all time
You'll try to kill me and I'll have no choice but to kill you
and in doing so I'll be killing my first grandchild. I don't want to do that.

ANAIA

O   my   god   where   am

I?

MAN

Anaia.
You came out so pretty. Be a pretty mother to your baby.
Come on. Put it down and I'll walk you down that hill and you'll go tell her whatever you need to tell her
and when that baby comes you'll bring it back

and I'll bounce it on my knee and we'll never talk about all the blood on the ground.
We'll brush it away like a cobweb.
Come on. I've got to bury my dead. We're the only ones left.

(Anaia lowers the sock. He goes to her and takes her hand gently.)

How far along are you?

ANAIA

Eleven weeks.

(He slaps her. Hard. She cradles her face, collapsing to the ground.)

MAN

That older one, the smart one, he was gonna be somebody.
Dog bitch.
If you weren't pregnant I'd cut your eyes out
and make you
eat
them.

(He kicks her and she tumbles down the hill.)

Go back to that h

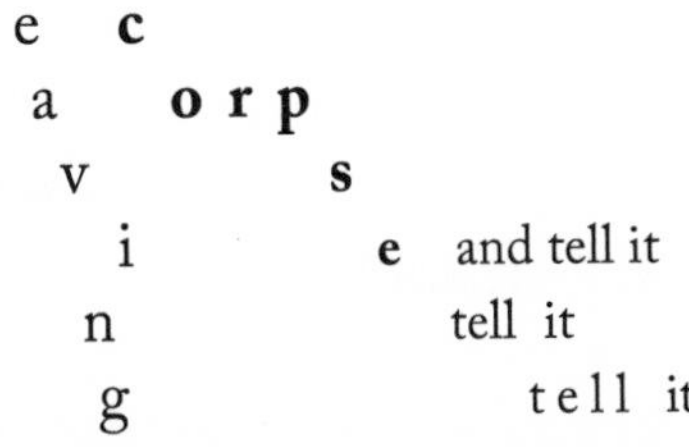

I'd do it a l l again
if i could

(Anaia struggles to stand. Man places the bodies of his sons near to one another. He takes a flask from his coat pocket and pours it on them.

Anaia has gotten to her feet. Man eyeballs her.)

ANAIA

While you was here whistling and making new babies and trying to forget all the bad things you did, Fourth Foster Mama was laughin at my scars with her friends.

MAN

I warned you.

ANAIA

Either you or me or somebody got to go today. World can't hold us both.

MAN

Suit yourself.

(He moves toward her but Racine jumps on his back.)

ANAIA

'Cine!

MAN

Get off me!

(Man is swinging around, trying to get Racine off his back.)

RACINE

Kill him, 'Naia!

(Anaia hits Man in the belly with the rock as hard as she can. He keels over. The twins descend on his fallen frame, kicking and stomping him. Racine takes the rock from her sister and brings it down on him repeatedly.)

You
ain't
n o t h i n
now

ANAIA

Yeah
Yeah
N o t h i n

RACINE

J
u n d
s o u
t r
a s o f t g
s p o t on the
Y o u
can't hit n o b o d y
can't H I T no body no more
can't set nobody on f i r e
can't marry some p r i ssy biiiitch
can't go have no new b a b i e s
can't hurt God you n o t h in

ANAIA AND RACINE

can't do n o b o d y like that you ain't N O T H I N
y o u the one thas wrong
crawl you down there grind crawl N O T H I N
monster ugly belly giant snake
you the one ain't 'bout shit N O T H I N
you the one that got left you you
what you gonna do now ain't N O T H I N
got no mama, no daddy no
place to put your feet up N O T H I N
you gon stay down you

(Racine takes the liquor and pours it all over Man's battered face. She takes his matches from the ground and strikes one.)

MAN

W a i t w a i t w a i t

RACINE

He
u l
g y,
ain't he, Twin?

ANAIA

Eyup.

(Racine drops the match, setting Man ablaze. He burns, writhes and screams.)

Let's go.

(The pair turn to leave, but Man grabs Racine's foot. The flame quickly travels up her leg.)

RACINE

Get off me,
mother
fucker!
Get off!
Let go!

ANAIA

'Cine?

(Racine cannot shake him off, though she fights hard. He pulls her closer. The flame engulfs her. She falls to the ground.)

RACINE

'Naia help get him off me 'Naia!

(Anaia takes a few steps back.)

'N a i a

(Anaia takes a few more steps back.)

ANAIA

i
i can't, Twin

RACINE

G e t   b u r n i n   G e t   T w i n   b u r n i n
h i m   T w i n   h i   m   i s ss   i s ss s
b u r n in iss iss is b u r n i nn iss s ss ssss b urnin iss ss sss
ssss s ss s s s s s s ssss s s s s s s s s ss s s s s s s s ssssss s s s s s s s

ANAIA

t'n a C

RACINE

Twin? T w i n? T
w n?
t w i n
w n ?
t

(Anaia runs and hides as her sister screams. The fire burns until everything is ash.)

TWIN?

Anaia makes her way from her hiding place.

ANAIA

Them b u r n i n
Them b u r n i n twi—
Anaia is too tired for this too tired she's too tired she's too tired for this
for this Twin
For this she's too tired
'Naia lookin out like somebody could see her without
f l i n c h i n g
she l o o k i n o u t

(Anaia looks out at us.)

She lower her head out of habit

(She leaves.)

AGAIN BEFORE GOD

Anaia stands before her mother, whose breath is coming in loose gasps. She is dwindling.

SHE

Well?

ANAIA

He's gone.

SHE

And your sister?

ANAIA

Her too.

(Anaia places the pieces of each of those killed before She—an ear, a manicured nail, Man's hat, etc.)

SHE

One, two, three, four, five.
Well, well. You did it.
I ain't tryna be funny, but I didn't think you'd be the one.

ANAIA

Yeah.

SHE

Reason you got burnt up worst is you was the one tryin hardest to save me. Guess that shoulda tol me something 'bout how dedicated you are.

ANAIA

Yeah

SHE

You alright, baby?

ANAIA

'Cine
'Cine died
and
and
you ain't even you ain't e'en

she dead, Mama. Dead.

He said . . . he told me you was the one . . .

SHE

What's that?

ANAIA

I got a baby comin. I'ma name it Enica. Thas almost Racine spelled backwards. Whatchoo think?

SHE

Clever.

(Anaia raises the rock-sock above her mother's head. She cannot see it.)

ANAIA

Mama
Mama   we cursed? Feel like it.

SHE

Hard to say.

ANAIA

Mama
You feel like you can die in peace, now?

SHE

Eyup. Iss real   q u i e t   now.

ANAIA

Funny
I still hear noise.

*(The almost imperceptible sound of a lullaby.
Anaia lowers the rock-sock to her side.)*

END

WHAT TO SEND UP WHEN IT GOES DOWN

A play. A pageant. A ritual. A homegoing celebration.

PRODUCTION HISTORY

What to Send Up When It Goes Down received its world premiere at the Harriet Tubman Center for Social Justice in Los Angeles, California, on November 13, 2015. It was directed by Aleshea Harris. The stage manager was Anthony Dawahare. The cast was: Jozben Barrett, DiJon-Delonté, Anthony Graham, Rebecka Jackson-Moeser, Carissa Pinckney, Arielle Siler, and Carol Simon.

What to Send Up When It Goes Down received its New York premiere by The Movement Theatre Company (David Mendizábal, Deadria Harrington, Eric Lockley, Taylor Reynolds, producing artistic leadership team) at A.R.T./New York Theatres on November 11, 2018. It was directed by Whitney White. The scenic design was by Yu-Hsuan Chen, the costume design was by Andy Jean, the lighting design was by Cha See, the sound design was by Sinan Refik Zafar; the production stage manager was Genevieve Ortiz. The cast was: Alana Raquel Bowers, Rachel Christopher, Ugo Chukwu, Kambi Gathesha, Naomi Lorrain, Denise Manning, Javon Q. Minter, and Beau Thom.

What to Send Up When It Goes Down has been performed at the Costume Shop at American Conservatory Theater, Occidental College, Boston Court Pasadena, Woolly Mammoth, A.R.T., BAM, and Playwrights Horizons.

HOW TO READ THIS PLAY

This play uses parody and absurdity to confront, to affirm, to celebrate.

The first section is a workshop carried out by the performers. It should be as informal and welcoming as possible.

The second section is experienced more traditionally, with the players presenting memorized text for any observers.

The margins are a space on the periphery of the main playing space. Whenever a figure "disappears" it is into the margins. That is, they remain but are barely visible.

The goal is healing through expression, expulsion, and movement. Have fun but don't play.

CAST

All Black. There may be doubling

ONE/MADE (W)
TWO (M)
THREE (W)
FOUR (W)
FIVE/MAN/DRIVER (M)
SIX/MISS (M)
SEVEN (M)
EIGHT (W)

Gender breakdown indicates what has happened in prior productions. I believe it works best if Miss, Driver and Made are portrayed by participants who identify with these specified gender designations as these roles draw on gendered tropes. All other roles are completely fluid.

FIRST MOVEMENT

Ideally, anyone viewing the ritual is waiting outside of the playing space. Four will make the following announcement:

FOUR

Welcome everyone.
I'm *(Name)* and on behalf of everyone involved I'd like to say that we are really pleased that you've decided to join us. I'd also like to clarify a couple of things before we get started so that everyone understands why we're here.
According to studies, Black people in America are more than twice as likely to be killed by police as white people.
This concerns us.
The officers responsible for these killings often go unpunished.
This concerns us.
As Black people, we must contend with living in a country which continually marginalizes and actively oppresses us. The

emotional and physiological toll of this concerns us and is the reason for this ritual.
Let me be clear: this ritual is first and foremost for Black people.
Again. We are glad non-Black people are here. We welcome you but this piece was created and is expressed with Black folks in mind. If you are prepared to honor that through your respectful, conscientious presence, you are welcome to stay.

Parts of the piece you're about to experience are participatory. Whether or not you choose to participate, be respectful. We are very serious about honoring real people who have died and offering strategies for those who need a way to heal.

Please also note that it is not often that Black people have a safe, public space for expressing their unfiltered feelings about anti-Blackness.
We are taking that space today.
Thank you.

(As the audience enters the space, they are each offered a black ribbon to pin to their clothing.)

TWO

Welcome everyone.
The black ribbon symbolizes our grief.
If you'd like a ribbon, please take one, put it on, and get into a circle.
If you are someone who is unable to stand for long periods of time, raise your hand and we can grab you a chair.

(Once everyone is settled, it continues.)

Thank you for joining us.
What we are about to carry out is a ritual honoring those lost to racist violence. If at any point during this ritual you find you

don't wish to do something that's been asked of you, please step out of the circle.
We only ask that you don't disrupt those participating in any way.

Let's start by sharing our names with each other. The way we're going to do it is whoever's turn it is, places their hand on their chest *(Demonstrates this)*, speaks their name, and then the next person does the same.

(This happens.)

Nice to meet you all.
We are here because many of us have been killed, but today in particular we're honoring *(Insert name of person recently killed)* who was killed on *(Insert date of killing)*.
(Name of deceased) was killed by more than the hands of *(Her/his/their)* killer.
(Name of deceased) was killed by an idea.
We think it's important to honor *(Name of deceased)* and to acknowledge that although *(Pronoun)* was killed by this idea, *(Pronoun)* was a person of value.

(Name of deceased) lived for *(Age of deceased upon death)* years. Let's honor *(Pronoun)* by speaking *(Pronoun)* name once for each year *(Pronoun)* lived.
One
(Name)
Two
(Name. Others will join. This continues until the number of years the person lived has been reached)

This idea, which we believe is partially responsible for the death of *(Name of deceased)*, is pretty pervasive in our culture.
It's so pervasive that I'm sure there's someone in this room who has heard someone say something anti-Black.

I'd like us to really consider that.
If you've ever heard someone say something racist about Black people firsthand, please step into the center of the circle.

(This happens.)

Good. Try and have a moment of awareness about who around you has stepped forward and who hasn't as we go through this exercise. Take a moment. Good. You can step back.

If there's anyone here who has ever seen someone be denied something:
a promotion, an opportunity to speak, or acknowledgment, for example.
If you feel you've ever witnessed someone being denied something because they are Black, please step forward.

(Following each prompt is a brief moment of quiet for reflection.)

Good.

Now, anyone who has ever felt they themselves have been denied something because you are Black:
an opportunity to speak, a fair contract, proper medical care, please step forward.

Now, let's talk about physical safety. Has anyone here ever seen someone physically threatened or assaulted and feel that it was because they were Black? If so, step forward.

If you've been physically threatened or assaulted and you believe it was because you are Black, step forward.

Now let's get even more specific, since the use of weapons by officers of the law have been such a big part of the conversation lately.

Have you ever seen someone be threatened or actually attacked by an officer of the law with some kind of weapon: a nightstick, a taser, pepper spray or a gun, and believe they wouldn't have been treated this way had they not been Black, step into the center.

You can step out.

Now if you yourself have been at the other end of a nightstick, pepper spray, a gun being wielded at you by an officer of the law and feel that being Black had something to do with it, please step into the center.

You can step out.

Now, let's each share one word that describes how we feel in this moment.
It can be any word you'd like to share.
We'll go around the circle again. Speak your word when it's your turn. Feel free to say "pass" if you wish.

Let's sit with that for a moment.

Now, we'll do the same thing, but this time we're going to share with each other a word that describes how we'd like to feel in this moment. We've said how we feel, now let's say how we would like to feel.

(This happens.)

Good.
Now, again, we're here to do many things, including celebrate the inherent value, the humanity of Black people since we are quite often dehumanized.

With this in mind, we'd like to extend an invitation to you.
Anyone here who feels they have some kind words they'd like to share with a Black person living in an anti-Black society, take a moment to write them down.
Take a few moments to do this.
Please be respectful. Do no further harm.

If you don't want to or can't for any reason, no one will give you a hard time.
We invite you to use this as a time for quiet reflection with yourself.
Once you've finished, please place them in the receptacles provided.

(They're given time to do this. Someone comes around with pens/small bits of paper and a bowl. The notes are dropped into a receptacle.)

When I get frustrated about these things, I find it really helpful to let it out with a yell. So, right now we're going to share a group yell as a strategy for releasing some of our negative feelings about the untimely death of *(Name of deceased)* together as a community. It can last as long as it needs to. As long as one of us is yelling, it's still happening. You can even take a breath and keep yelling if you need to. Close your eyes. On the count of three. One, two, three . . .

(Group yell happens. A beat.)

Good. Breath is a great equalizer, isn't it? We all need to take it to stay alive. Each of us is making use of it as I speak these words. Right now as a community unique to this very moment, let's take a collective breath on the count of three.
One, two, three.

(They do.)

Let's do that again.

(They do.)

And one last time.

(They do.)

Now, some of us are going to continue with another part of the ritual but we need your help getting there.
In order to launch us into the next part of this thing, we need song, a bridge between this moment and our next.
You could think of this song as fuel.
We're going to teach it to you and we hope that you'll join us in singing it.

Here we go.

(Eight teaches song:)

EIGHT

SUN COME UP
SHINE ON ME
CAN'T STOP IT
FEELIN FREE

AND I GOT THAT LOVE
FROM BELOW AND ABOVE
FROM THE LEFT AND RIGHT

ON EVERY SIDE

WANNA THANK YOU
WANNA THANK YOU
WANNA THANK YOU . . .

(After a couple times through . . .)

TWO

Good.
Now, let's join hands and sing it all together as a way to honor *(Name of deceased)*, our community and our cause.

(They sing through it maybe twice. As everyone sings, the members of the ensemble begin to drift away from the circle one by one, preparing for the next part of the ritual. When it feels right, Two speaks.)

Let's keep singing as we make our way to our seats.

(Once the viewers are seated, Two resumes.)

The People are coming because it is the day after or the day before it has gone down.

You know what I mean by "it," right?
"It" equals some terrible thing.
Some "bang-bang" thing.
Some wrong color thing.
The shit that don't stop.

Since it don't stop
we are always before and after it going down.
You feel me?
It happened yesterday and it will happen tomorrow
We find ourselves between the happenings.

Stay with me.

It is the year *(Insert date and year)* and we are right here at *(Name of venue)* on stolen *(Name of Indigenous peoples who once held the land)* land.

But it is of also circa 1900, in some unknown city
in these united states,
what's left of the "unknown negro" propped up
in an old wooden chair
the insides of his head outside
the outsides of his head caved inside
and it is also May 16th, 1916 in Waco, Texas,
the smell still smelling
and it is of course September 30th, 1919 in Arkansas,
the screams still slicing through the air.
You get the picture.
The shame of the picture, plus the fuckery of shit having gone down and the knowing that it will go down again will not allow for the mincing of words or giving of too many fucks about delicate sensibilities or convention.
It don't make sense, so why should it make sense?
On your marks
Get set
Bang!

(Eight beats a rhythm into her chest as she sings:)

EIGHT

MAMA HAD A ROSEBUSH
IN THE GARDEN
DADDY HAD A SHIP
THAT SAILED THE SEA
I'M LOOKIN ALL AROUND
FOR WHAT I'M HOLDIN
DON'T SEE NOTHING BUT ME

ME ON THE SIDEWALK
ME ON THE FENCE
AM I GOIN CRAZY
IT DON'T MAKE NO SENSE

SEARCHIN FOR THAT GARDEN
UNDERGROUND
WENT HUNTING FOR THAT
HIDDEN TREASURE—ALMOST DROWNED

MAMA WHERE'D YOU HIDE THAT ROSEBUSH
DADDY WHY'D YOU SINK THAT SHIP
I GOT NOTHIN TO PUT IN MY JEWELRY BOX
AND I'M FEELIN A LITTLE SICK

ALL

O

EIGHT

MAMA WON'T YOU TAKE MY TEMPERATURE
DADDY WON'T YOU FILL THIS SCRIPT
TRYNA GET WELL, TRYNA GET WELL
BEFORE I ABSOLUTELY LOSE MY SHHHHHH . . .

(The performers hurriedly go to their places in the margins. Meanwhile, the actors portraying Made, Man and Miss transform into their respective characters. Made wears an apron, Man wears a limo driver's hat. Miss may put on a hat and pearls, etc.
The tempo of "Fixing Miss" must be clipped. Vaudeville-esque.)

TWO

The People prepare to say what needs saying.

MADE

"Fixing Miss": A play within a play.
Characters: Made, that's "M-A-D-E"—a woman of her own devising. Made stands at a table sharpening a knife.

MAN

Man. A man weary of the margins. He stands at attention.

MISS

Miss enters. She is white and has a Southern dialect not unlike Paula Deen's. She is old and generally jittery.

MAN

As soon as Miss enters, Man becomes Driver, breaking his stillness to tend to her.
Driver performs Miss's favorite negro dialect:
Miss, Miss, whatchoo need, Miss? I gotchoo, Miss. Anythang you missed, I'ma get for ya, Miss. Whatcha need?

MISS

I don't need anything from you.
I am wealthy and white and liberated.
My hands are clean.
I am wealthy and white
So wealthy and white that I don't need anything from you.

DRIVER

But . . . uh, Miss, I'll do anything for to make you happy! Thas what I'm here for!

MISS

O, hush up.

DRIVER

I needs me some purpose, Miss.

MISS

(Enjoying this) O, stop.

DRIVER

I could frame ya, if ya want. Black is a real good color for a frame. I can do anything to make ya feel good about yoself. It'd be my privilege—

MISS

"Privilege"? Don't you start about privilege. Why, I've worked for everything I've ever gotten.

DRIVER

Yes'm . . . what I mean is I'm real happy to be some kinda vehicle fo yo edificamation. I needs my purpose up in this here play, otherwise I'm jus gon slide right offa the character list and into the margins, and I doan wanna do that!

MISS

Not my problem.

DRIVER

I means it, Miss, I means it! Gimme somethin to do!

MISS

What you do with yourself is none of my concern. My hands are clean.

(Driver bends over backward.)

DRIVER

I'll bend over backward! See! See! See!

MISS

You are making a fool of yourself—

(Driver begins to slide into the margins.)

DRIVER

Please! Please! I'm bein sucked into the margins, Miss!

(Miss watches him go. A moment. Then . . .)

MISS

O, alright. Come on back.

(Driver is back in a flash.)

DRIVER

Thank you, Miss!

MISS

I spose I could use a seat.

(Driver happily gets on all fours. She sits on him.)

But don't think this means I need you. I can get rid of you whenever I please. You are a luxury.

DRIVER

Yes'm.

MISS

My hands are clean.

DRIVER

Yes'm.

MISS

(Quietly) You don't steal, do you?

DRIVER

No'm.

MISS

Good. Calling you out for stealing would make me look mean and racist and I am neither mean nor racist. What I am is wealthy, white, and liberated.

DRIVER

'Course you is.

MISS

My hands are clean.

DRIVER

Yes'm.

MISS

Now take me over to the maid.

DRIVER

(Forgetting "negro dialect") Shall I sing a negro spiritual as I do?

MISS

What?

DRIVER

Shall I sing a—

MISS

I don't understand a word you're saying.

DRIVER

(Back to "negro dialect") I mean, you be wantin me to sing one of my colored songs, Missus, while I be carryin you around? We real good at makin music!

MISS

No. Your shucking and jiving and driving are sufficient.

DRIVER

He carries her to Made

MADE

Who is still sharpening the knife.

MISS

What are you doing?

MADE

Kneading flour.

MISS

O. Making fresh bread, are we?

MADE

Yes, we are.

MISS

Hm.

(She taps Driver and he carries her away.)

Did you hear that?

DRIVER

Yes'm.

MISS

She was a bit impudent, wasn't she?

DRIVER

Yes'm.

MISS

And I'm not entirely sure about that bread she's making. I am gluten-free, and I am certain she is not taking care to remove all of the gluten.

DRIVER

You prolly right.

MISS

You can't pull one over on me. I am a friend to your kind but that does not make me a fool.

DRIVER

No'm. It don't.

MISS

That look in her eyes was very telling.

DRIVER

What did it tell you, Miss?

MISS

Something about fire, a schoolhouse, and ghosts. That mean anything to you?

DRIVER

No'm. But—

MISS

I try to understand the struggle. I see the movies. I saw *The Help*, the *Roots* (both the original and the reboot), the *Selma*, the *Green Book*, the *When They See Us*, and the *Black Panther* to boot.

DRIVER

Yes'm—

MISS

And I have Black friends. We're friends, aren't we?

DRIVER

Tha besta friends. You lets me listen to all your troubles.

MISS

You are not slaves. You work of your own free will.

DRIVER

Yes'm. Y'all let us do whatever we want. White House or jailhouse or—

MISS

Your choice.

DRIVER

Yes'm. And issa privilege to be up under you—

MISS

What's that? Privilege? I am not some trust-fund ninny I have worked for everything that is mine privilege had nothing to do with it! Now take me over to the maid! I want to non-racistly assert myself as her boss but not as a racist.

DRIVER

Yes'm. Dis here yo story—

He carries her over to Made.

MADE

Who is now loading a bow and arrow.

MISS

Hello there.
Hi.
Hi?

(Miss looks to Driver for help. He shrugs.)

How-what-how's your day going?

MADE

Fine.

MISS

What are you up to?

MADE

Laundry.

MISS

O. That's nice.
Why are you doing laundry at this hour?

MADE

Why not?

MISS

Well, it's a strange hour for laundry. Wouldn't you like to take tea with me? We could talk about our kids. I'm sure they've got lots in common.

MADE

I don't have any kids.

MISS

Really?

MADE

Really.

MISS

Are you planning on having—

MADE

If you don't mind, I'm needed doing this laundry.

MISS

Well. I do mind. I'm trying to have a conversation with you. Get to know you. You've been employed here for quite some time and I think we should become acquainted, so put that laundry down and let's talk.

MADE

We can talk but I can't stop with this laundry.

MISS

Fine. Well. I'll start.
I enjoy brunch. And church and my work, which is the care of children. All kinds of children.
You?
Ahem.
What do you like—

MADE

I really don't want to mess up and put the lights with the darks. If you'll excuse me.

MISS

I—I—okay.

(Pats Driver who takes her away.)

I am troubled. This is troubling.
I think I'll have to let her go.

DRIVER

O.

MISS

What?

DRIVER

Huh?

MISS

You—

DRIVER

Whah?

MISS

What's that?

DRIVER

Nothin—

MISS

Well?

DRIVER

Naw—

MISS

I—

DRIVER

Nuh-uh—

MISS

What do you mean by saying that? Am I to keep an insolent worker?

DRIVER

No'm, but—

MISS

Am I to put up with someone who can't be bothered to make friends with me?
I do wonder what, if you'll pardon the expression, crawled up her butt!

I am a friend to you all but that does not mean that I have to tolerate sass!
I non-racistly assert the right to have whichever colored maid I like!

DRIVER

Yes'm.

MISS

What?

DRIVER

Nothin.

MISS

Do you—

DRIVER

No'm—

MISS

What's that look about? I don't owe her anything.
Take me back over there right this instant!

DRIVER

You da boss!

MISS

Wait! I'm not going anywhere.
Ahem.
You. Maid. What are you doing?

MADE

Made is oiling a machete. She does not even look at Miss.
(To Miss) Sweeping.

MISS

Put down that broom and come here.

MADE

I'm needed sweeping.

MISS

You are needed where I say you are needed I can do my own sweeping I grew up doing my own sweeping I never needed anyone to do it for me I grew up poor You are a luxury My hands are clean Please come over here.

MADE

Made goes to Miss, hips first.

MISS

Your sass of late has become too much for me to handle It's just gotten out of hand Too much Way overboard. Have you got anything to say for yourself?

MADE

Made answers with her shoulders. *(A shrug)*

MISS

Are you going through some sort of private crisis—

MADE

Nope.

MISS

If you were having some issue—

MADE

Nope—

MISS

I understand and am sympathetic—

MADE

No issue—

MISS

Maybe one of your kids is sick—

(Made slaps Miss.)

MADE

Made slaps the shit out of Miss.

(Miss continues as if she hadn't noticed.)

MISS

Maybe one of your kids is sick and you're needing some time off—

(Made slaps Miss again. Again, Miss continues as if she hadn't noticed.)

You're needing some time off to tend to your little ones. I can understand that.

MADE

I don't have any fucking kids you witless cunt!
Made punches Miss.

(Punches, but Miss isn't affected. She shakes her head, confused.)

MISS

You seem upset.

MADE

Made cannot stop hitting Miss.

(Miss looks to Driver—who shrugs his shoulders.)

MISS

You must be having a bad day—

(Made kisses Miss squarely on the mouth. Miss mimes the actions; she describes it, dying a hilarious, dramatic death.)

Miss is horrified, reacts as if she's been shot, stabbed, punched.
She screams, moans, and rages, ending up on the floor.
You—You—You! Are! Fired!!

(Miss is very still.)

MADE AND MAN

O. shit.

(Three enters from the margins with a bowl filled with shredded white paper. She drops bits of the paper on the ground as she speaks, moving throughout the space.)

THREE

Do you remember when I tried to love you?
You and you stood with me in a circle at a party
on a boat, in a roaring house by a fire
in a log cabin and we breathed the same air but not really
yours seemed bigger and though I stood with you and you in that tight circle
you and you let a truth tumble out of your mouth
which put me in Africa with a bone in my nose
doing a nigger dance
which put me in The Ghetto looking suspicious
and being suspiciously quite nigger-ly
you and you put me beneath your boots
or in the cupboard or in the corner of your eyes, platoon, spelling bee—

(Four and Eight appear.)

EIGHT

So, I tried to, like, be cool about it, you know.
Ever since I read that psychotherapy book, I'm all into my breath and checking in with my body and stuff, you know?

FOUR

I feel you.

EIGHT

But he was pissed. You know that really special nobody-ever-dares-call-me-on-my bullshit, especially-not-some-black bitch way white men get pissed?

FOUR

I know it very well.

EIGHT

So, I'm going in like I do, tryna explain things calmly, you know—

FOUR

O, Lord. What'd he say?

EIGHT

He looked at me and said . . .
He doesn't see color . . .

(They freak out, running all over the room, laughing. Maybe they "shout," à la a person stricken with the Holy Ghost. Twerk incredulously. Some amused/shocked expression of "Lord, help me not to slap somebody.")

FOUR

No the hell he didn't.

EIGHT

Yes the hell he did.

FOUR

No, his ass didn't.

EIGHT

Yes, his ass did.

FOUR

What'd you say?

EIGHT

I didn't say anything.

FOUR

Nothing?

EIGHT

What could I say?

FOUR

I can think of a few things.

EIGHT

Nah. I'm tired. I just politely leaned forward in my chair . . .

FOUR

Mm hm.

EIGHT

and took his mouth.

FOUR

What?

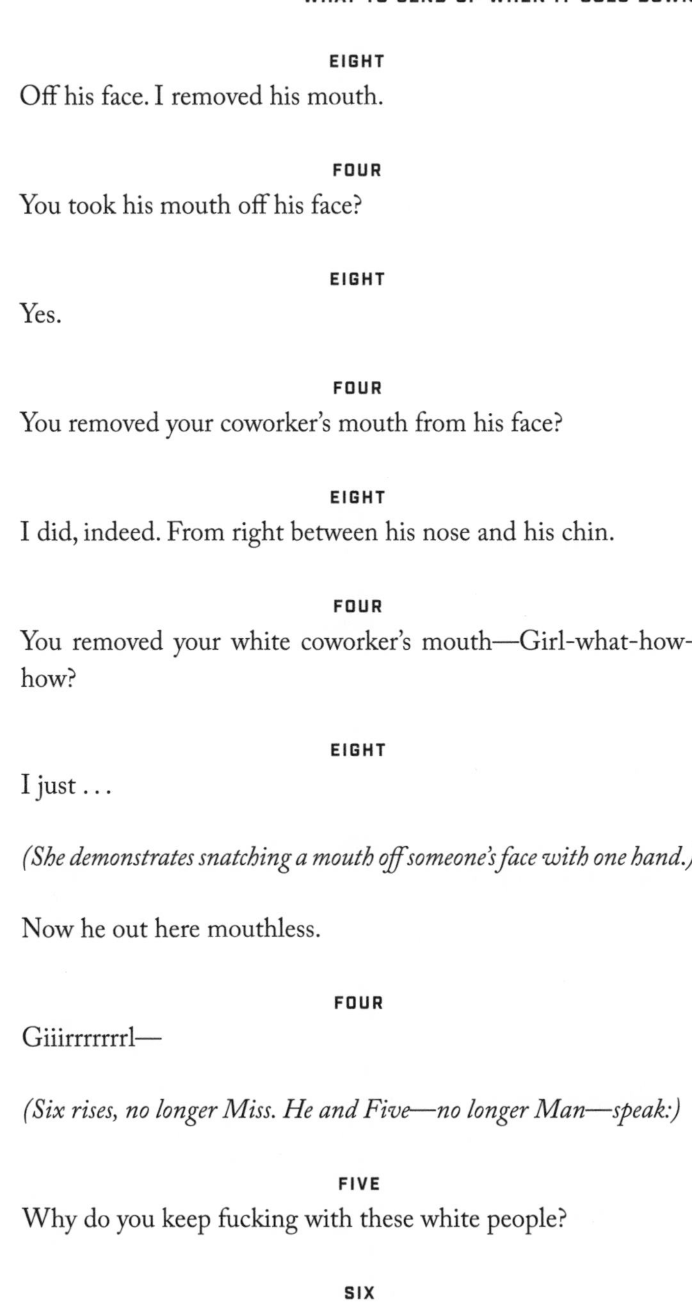

EIGHT

Off his face. I removed his mouth.

FOUR

You took his mouth off his face?

EIGHT

Yes.

FOUR

You removed your coworker's mouth from his face?

EIGHT

I did, indeed. From right between his nose and his chin.

FOUR

You removed your white coworker's mouth—Girl-what-how-how?

EIGHT

I just . . .

(She demonstrates snatching a mouth off someone's face with one hand.)

Now he out here mouthless.

FOUR

Giiirrrrrrrl—

(Six rises, no longer Miss. He and Five—no longer Man—speak:)

FIVE

Why do you keep fucking with these white people?

SIX

What do you mean?

FIVE

You fuck with them.

SIX

I fux with everybody.

FIVE

You tryna be funny?

SIX

Maybe.

FIVE

Do you want to die?

SIX

C'mon—

FIVE

You do, don't you?

SIX

Is that a real question?

FIVE

You have a death wish.

SIX

Suicide by white person. Is that a thing?

FIVE

I'm serious.

SIX

Chill, bruh. They fuck with me and I respond in kind.

FIVE

If you don't want to die, quit responding!
And quit walking down the street.

SIX

You don't want me to walk down the street?

FIVE

No.

SIX

I can't walk down the street?

FIVE

No, you can't.
Especially not with the way you walk down the street.

SIX

The way?

FIVE

Yes, the way.

SIX

And what way is that?

FIVE

You know.

SIX

I don't. I'm curious. Like, how do I do it?

FIVE

Brazenly.
In their neighborhoods.
Brazenly!
You know they hate that.

SIX

But show me though.
Show me how I do it.

FIVE

You do it all like this.

(Five imitates Six walking down a street. It is a normal walk.)

SIX

Like that? That's how I do it?

FIVE

That's exactly how you do it!

SIX

O, 'cause I thought I was more like . . .

(Six does this ridiculous pimp-daddy walk, complete with gang signs and maybe even ends with a jailhouse pose.)

I thought that was how I did it.

FIVE

No, no. You definitely do it like this:

(Five demonstrates the normal walk again.)

And then you be all like,
"Hi." Like that. Like y'all are pals.

SIX

We're not pals?

FIVE

No. You and white people are not pals.

SIX

Homies?

FIVE

No.

SIX

Confidants—

FIVE

God. No!

SIX

Alright! Damn.

(Seven appears.)

SEVEN

Daddy used to say,
"*(Name of actor)*, you don't get to be foolish, too, boy.
You already Black. Don't add Fool to the equation.
Foolish Black folks get swept off their feet in the worst way.
Foolish Black folks get cheated out of their own skin and bone.
Foolish Black folk come to this world like rabbits
and get taken out like trash.
Black and foolish is the last thing you wanna be.
You can be uppity, you can be a ho but you bet not, bet not be foolish."
So, Fool ain't in me.
Uh uh.
It ain't in my food, my walk or my attire.
You will not find Fool in the gin I drink,
under my fingernails or in my speech.
Let them be foolish
I am very Black and very much the picture of perfection

I keeps it sharp.
If you say you seen Fool anywhere on *(Name of actor)*'s person,
you. a muthafuckin. lie.

(Four enters the space holding the bowl of white shredded paper.)

FOUR

When I say "Black people," I want you to say, "yeah."
Black people

ALL

Yeah.

FOUR

Black people.

ALL

Yeah.

FOUR

Black people.

ALL

Yeah!

FOUR

A lot of times when people call your name like that, a lot of times when they say "Black" they're saying something bad about you. Am I right, Black people?

ALL

Yeah.

FOUR

Big Black people

ALL

Yeah.

FOUR

Loud Black people

ALL

Yeah.

FOUR

Angry Black people

ALL

Yeah.

FOUR

Stupid Black people

ALL

Yeah.

FOUR

Ugly Black people

ALL

Yeah.

FOUR

Poor Black people

ALL

Yeah.

FOUR

Criminal Black people

ALL

Yeah.

FOUR

Too many kids havin Black people

ALL

Yeah.

FOUR

Fat Black people

ALL

Yeah.

FOUR

Lazy Black people

ALL

Yeah.

FOUR

Ghetto Black people

ALL

Yeah.

FOUR

Urban (Black people)

ALL

Yeah.

FOUR

Sassy Black people

ALL

Yeah.

FOUR

Entitled-ass Black people

ALL

Yeah.

FOUR

Not even worth mentioning Black people

ALL

Yeah

FOUR

Synonymous with "slave" Black people

ALL

Yeah

FOUR

You best behave Black people

ALL

Yeah

FOUR

Dead Black people

ALL

Yeah

FOUR

Dead for bein Black Black people

ALL

Yeah

FOUR

Your bodies are dangerous Black people

ALL

Yeah

FOUR

You are walking weapons Black people

ALL

Yeah

FOUR

You got some weight on you Black people

ALL

Yeah

FOUR

You ready to unpack Black people?

ALL

Yeah

FOUR

Drop somethin!

(They drop bits of paper slowly as Three enters, dropping more paper.)

THREE

You lookin at me like "what"?
You lookin at me like "whoa"

Like "whoa" Like "what" Like "whoa"
What
What
What
When so many words are fighting their way out of my mouth that it foams
You and you don't want to listen to the words themselves
preferring, instead, to ponder the foam's density and viscosity like,
"Where did it come from? Why she so mad?"
Well, I just don't know.
I guess there was a sale on Mad down at the Mad Store
So I went down and bought me some Mad
And, here it is.
Meanwhile, I and I can't find myself in the mirror, in the reflection of the screen
unless of course I am biting myself.
You and you approve of the biting of the self
especially when it is a self that looks like me
You love it, O, you love it when I bite myself
because that is the kind of Black story you like.
When I am heavy and downtrodden
with biting myself
when I wear the flavor of Blackness you like
When it is warm and fuzzy Blackness that does not creep under your bedroom door at night
Blackness that doesn't disrupt brunch or make you question
the things your privilege steals and steals from me
O, you love it
You wield your pen
I blubber most Blackly
You nod your head, you know this story
I weep, I moan, I reach for you from down below
You love it
You wield your pen most bravely
You are afraid to come to my neighborhood

You would never help my aunt with her groceries
You do not see me coming
but you come see my story
You sit in your soft chair
You review me and you do not feel the foolishness of it
You feel no shame
You really think you are in charge
I'd be embarrassed for you if I weren't so busy fighting for my life
If I were to turn my teeth toward you
If I were to turn my teeth toward you
You and you would not know what to do and do
Do you do you
Do you remember when I tried to love you?
Do you remember when I tried to love you?
It was like riding a bike without a chain.

FIVE

Brazenly.

SIX

What?

FIVE

You walk around in their neighborhoods.
Brazenly!
You know they hate that.

SIX

Not their neighborhoods.
Not their streets.
Everything they got, they stole.
Streets and people
Streets and people
But they ain't got me.

FIVE

If they got guns, they got you.

SIX

Naw.

FIVE

The judge and the senators they got—

SIX

Naw.

FIVE

The police, they got.
Time and the law, they got.
They got you.

SIX

Naw.

FIVE

You keep on. You'll find out.

SIX

Whatever.

(Six makes to leave.)

FIVE

Where you going?

SIX

To one of "their" houses.

FIVE

Don't be stupid.

SIX

Gotta take a leak. Gonna water the azaleas.

FIVE

That isn't funny.
Stop laughing.

SIX

A brotha can't even laugh?

FIVE

You don't have to do it the way you do it
In their faces
loud and wide
showing all your teeth
you laugh like—

SIX

You're right, I do.
But those crackas deserve it.

FIVE

O my god, you must really want to die.

SEVEN

So when they shoot another one of us, I come up with a plan.
I get a razor and cut a straight line, not too deep, just deep enough to do the trick.
I cut from the navel to the sternum
and then two more lines from the sternum out to the shoulders.
A "Y"
like how they cut the dead ones open.
I figure if I already look dead, there ain't nothin for them to kill.
Iss like playin possum.
You see? Sharp.

EIGHT

Don't look at me like that.

FOUR

A white man's mouth? Just . . . just like that?

EIGHT

Just took it off his face.

FOUR

O my god! Was anyone else there?

EIGHT

O yeah. Other people were there. My supervisor's jaw hit the floor. They got all wide in the eyes, like "*(Name of actor)*'s gone crazy." I put that mouth in my purse and left.

FOUR

No one tried to stop you?

EIGHT

Now you know good and well they were scared.

FOUR

What does it look like?

EIGHT

Like a little fish flopping around. Look.

(She opens her purse but not for long, lest the mouth jump out.)

FOUR

That's disgusting.

EIGHT

I know. It won't shut up, either.

FOUR

What's it saying?

EIGHT

The usual. Something about my neck.

FOUR

They're gonna come after you.
With fire, they'll come.

EIGHT

And I'll be here with this mouth. Let 'em come.

FOUR

Girl.

EIGHT

Tired.

SEVEN

I strut down the street
with this "Y" so neat and pretty
lookin like a muthafuckin superhero
Don't need no cape or nothing.
Naw, don't need no cape.
All I gotta do is—shit.

(Seven smarts. A sharp pain from the "Y" on his chest)

The fuck?

THREE

I and I beamed my least nigger-ly smile and offered you a beer
and you took the beer but would not let our fingers touch
I pretended not to notice—

bigger-ing my non-nigger smile but you got scared or horny
You told me, you tell me a story
about someone you love who hates me
You say,
"My uncle is a bit racist but you must understand that he is from a different time."
And so the arrowhead is in me
not you nor your uncle
me
I try to take it out gingerly—I try
This is an office function, after all
It wouldn't do to walk around with an arrow in my back—

SEVEN

This ain't my Y. This Y's got fresh blood. And it feels like I'm all hollowed out—

THREE

Arrow in my back—

SEVEN

Iss enough ghosts up in here.

(All take an audible breath and run to the margins, save for Two, who speaks to the audience.)

SECOND MOVEMENT

This second time around, all action occurs a bit more quickly than the last time.

TWO

The People are coming because it is the day after or the day before it has gone down.

You know what I mean by "it," right?
"It" equals some terrible thing.
Some "bang-bang" thing.
Some wrong color thing.
The shit that don't stop.
Since it don't stop
we are always before and after it going down.
We find ourselves between the happenings.

Stay with me.

It is the year *(Insert date and year)* and we are right here in *(Name of theater/space/side of town).*
And it is also July 19th, 1935 in Fort Lauderdale, Florida, the little girls chewing taffy and watching the swing, swing, swing.
And it is also June 16th, 1944 in Columbus, South Carolina, the boy going into the death house.
And it is of course August 28th, 1955, the Tallahatchie River fuller than usual.

You get the picture.

The shame of the picture, plus the fuckery of shit having gone down and the knowing that it will go down again
will not allow for the giving of too many fucks.

It don't make sense, so why should it make sense?
On your marks
Get set
Bang!

EIGHT

ME ON THE SIDEWALK
ME ON THE FENCE
AM I GOIN CRAZY

IT DON'T MAKE NO SENSE
SEARCHIN FOR THAT GARDEN
UNDERGROUND
WENT HUNTING FOR THAT
HIDDEN TREASURE—ALMOST DROWNED

MAMA WHERE'D YOU HIDE THAT ROSEBUSH
DADDY WHY'D YOU SINK THAT SHIP
I GOT NOTHIN TO PUT IN MY JEWELRY BOX
AND I'M FEELIN A LITTLE SICK

ALL

O

EIGHT

MAMA WON'T YOU TAKE MY TEMPERATURE
DADDY WON'T YOU FILL THIS SCRIPT
TRYNA GET WELL, TRYNA GET WELL
BEFORE I ABSOLUTELY LOSE MY SHHHHHH . . .

(A flurry as performers head to the margins.
As this happens, the actors portraying Made, Man and Miss reset for the beginning of the following section. The tempo of "Fixing Miss" must be even more clipped and the performances more intensified.)

TWO

The People prepare to say it.

MADE

"Fixing Miss:" A play within a play
Characters: "M-A-D-E"—a woman of her own devising.
Made stands at a table, loading a revolver.

MAN

Man. A man weary of the margins. Flexible. He stands at attention.

MISS

Miss enters. She is white, pearls, pantsuit, degrees, jittery.

MAN

As soon as Miss enters, Man becomes Driver, performing Miss's favorite negro dialect:
Miss, Miss, whatcha need, Miss? Anythang you missed, I'ma get for ya, Miss. Whatcha need?

MISS

Don't need anything from you.
Liberated and educated.
So liberated and educated that I don't need anything from you.

DRIVER

But . . . uh, Miss, I'll do anything for to make you happy!

MISS

O, hush.

DRIVER

Need me some purpose—

MISS

O, stop.

DRIVER

I could frame ya, if ya want. I'm frame-colored. It'd be my privilege—

MISS

Don't you start about privilege.

DRIVER

Yes ma'am . . . I need me a purpose up in this here play, otherwise I'm jus gonna slide right off the character list and into the margins—

MISS

Not my problem.

DRIVER

I mean it, Miss. Gimme somethin to do!

MISS

None of my concern.

(Driver begins to slide into the margins)

DRIVER

I'm bein sucked into the margins, Miss!

(Miss watches him go. A moment.)

MISS

O, come on back.

(Driver is back in a flash.)

DRIVER

Thank you, Miss!

MISS

No slouching. Stand up straight.
(He does so)
Not too straight.

DRIVER

Huh?

MISS

Just. Please. My feet are tired.

(Driver happily gets on all fours. She sits on him.)

But don't think this means I need you.

DRIVER

Yes ma'am.

MISS

My hands are clean.

DRIVER

Yes ma'am.

MISS

(Quietly) You don't . . . have a record, do you?

DRIVER

No ma'am.

MISS

Good. Firing you for having a record would make me look mean and racist.

DRIVER

'Course.

MISS

My hands are clean.

DRIVER

Yes ma'am.

MISS

Now take me over to the housekeeper.

DRIVER

He carries her to Made

MADE

Who is still loading those bullets into that revolver.

MISS

What are you doing?

MADE

Shelling peas.

MISS

Those don't look like peas.
Exotic?

MADE

Yes.

(She taps Driver and he carries her away.)

MISS

You hear that?

DRIVER

Yes ma'am.

MISS

Bit of an attitude.

DRIVER

Yes ma'am.

MISS

Had an attitude with Mama, too.

DRIVER

Uh huh.

MISS

And something is not right about those peas.

DRIVER

No ma'am.

MISS

That look in her eyes.

DRIVER

Yup.

MISS

I try my best. I'm one of the good ones.

DRIVER

Yup.

MISS

Should I be treated like trash just because you all have been oppressed?

DRIVER

Uh . . . ?

MISS

My hands are clean.

DRIVER

Sho nuff. You 'bout the nicest white lady—

MISS

Hush. Got to focus.
Something's off-kilter here.
You feel it?

DRIVER

This yo story—

MISS

Take me back over there. I am going to assert myself non-racistly.

(Driver takes her over to Made, who mimes cleaning the chamber of a machine gun.)

MADE

Made is now cleaning the chamber of a machine gun.

MISS

How-what-how's your day going?

MADE

Fine.

MISS

What are you up to?

MADE

Scrubbing the bathtub.

MISS

Strange hour for scrubbing
We could talk about our kids. I'm sure they've got lots in common.

MADE

I don't have any kids.

MISS

Really? Mama said you had—

MADE

Really.

MISS

Are you planning on having—

MADE

If you don't mind, I'm needed scrubbing this tub.

MISS

I'm trying to have a conversation with you. You've been in the family for years. Let's talk.

MADE

We can talk but I can't stop scrubbing.

MISS

I'll start.
I enjoy brunch, church, and children.
What do you like—

MADE

Don't want to mess up and miss a spot. Excuse me.

MISS

Okay.

(Pats Driver who takes her away.)

I'll have to let her go.

DRIVER

O.

MISS

What?

DRIVER

Huh?

MISS

That was—

DRIVER

What—

MISS

Huh?

DRIVER

I don't—

MISS

Am I to keep a maid with an attitude problem?

DRIVER

No ma'am, but—

MISS

I non-racistly assert the right to have whichever one of y'all that I like!

DRIVER

Yes ma'am.

MISS

What?

DRIVER

Nothin.

MISS

Huh?

DRIVER

What?

MISS

She has other options, doesn't she?

DRIVER

Y'all done gave—

MISS

Take me back over there so I can fire her.

DRIVER

You the boss!

MISS

Wait!
Ahem.
You. Housekeeper. What are you doing?

MADE

Made is aiming a rocket launcher. She does not even look at Miss.
Vacuuming.

MISS

Put down that vacuum and come here.

MADE

I'm needed vacuuming.

MISS

You are needed where I say you are needed.
You are a luxury. My hands are clean. Come over here.

MADE

Made puts down the rocket launcher.

MISS

Your sass has gotten out of hand.
Have you got anything to say?

MADE

What?

MISS

Are you going through a private crisis—

MADE

Nope.

MISS

Having some issue—

MADE

Nope—

MISS

I'm sympathetic—

MADE

No issue—

MISS

Maybe one of your kids is sick—

(Made slaps Miss.)

MADE

Made slaps the shit out of Miss.

(Miss continues as if she hadn't noticed.)

MISS

Maybe one of your kids is sick and—

(Made slap Miss again. Again, Miss continues as if she hadn't noticed.)

You're needing some time off. I can understand that.

MADE

I don't have any fucking kids you witless cunt!

MISS

You seem upset. If you'll apologize for your attitude today—

MADE

Made cannot stop!

(Made continues hitting Miss, to no avail.)

MISS

Woman troubles, I presume. Not making use of one's womb will do that to—

(Made kisses Miss square on the mouth.)

Miss is horrified, reacts as if she's been shot, stabbed, punched.
She screams, moans, and rages, ending up on the floor.
You—You—You! Are! Fired!!

(Miss is dead.)

MADE AND MAN

O. shit.

THREE

I tried to love you, I tried.
I tried to laugh with you but it sounded wrong.
It was all jittery. It was all jittery because of your joke about how many Black people it takes to screw in a light bulb or how all the Black girls dance or whatever funny joke they're telling about Black people these days.
I looked down and realized joke was on me
literally, all over me
and in me.

The kids were laughing. All of their pink faces laughing.
Teacher was trying to hide a titter behind her hand.
I do a little dance as I run back to the ghetto hoping I don't look too suspicious or particularly ready to die—

EIGHT

You were right about them coming
You were right and now
Won't nothing straighten out my neck
Can't seem to
Straighten out my neck
Took a crane to it

FOUR

Prayed

EIGHT

Took a hammer to it

FOUR

Prayed

EIGHT

Got a brace for it. Wept and wailed

FOUR

Prayed

EIGHT

Got on the news and shook the man's hand.
Said it was okay, was gonna be okay

FOUR

Told people to pray
Stopped the blood from coming out of my lover's body with my mouth
Plugged it up

EIGHT AND FOUR

The camera rolling the whole time.

EIGHT

My spine doesn't riot, my arms aren't raised.

FOUR

Held hands with the other mothers
Pinned a flower to me

EIGHT

Picked up the baby and the entrails they cut out
All in the dust. Picked them up

FOUR

Took the thing from 'round my neck—

EIGHT

and ankles

FOUR

You ever try to kiss someone but you can't
'cause you're too crooked?

EIGHT

Yeah. All the time. My ex used to tell me I tasted like copper.

FOUR

How does he know what copper tastes like?

EIGHT

Girrrrrrrrrl.

SEVEN

This ain't my Y.
Somebody else made this one

This Y is bleeding like a fresh cut.
This Y got stitches in it.
And I can't find my insides.
I'm missing my insides like how the dead ones is missing their insides—

FIVE

You fux with white people?

SIX

Huh?

FIVE

With white people. You fux with them?

SIX

Naw, homey. Well. From time to time.

FIVE

Why?

SIX

Why?

FIVE

Yeah, why?

SIX

'Cause all god's children needs to be fucked with.

(They laugh.)

FIVE

How do you fuck with them?

SIX

Like this.

(He walks normally.)

FIVE

You do that?

SIX

Hell yeah!

FIVE

In public?

SIX

Hell, hell yeah.

FIVE

You crazy.
You got white friends?

SIX

Eyup.

FIVE

For real?

SIX

Eyup.

FIVE

How many?

SIX

I got so many white friends.

FIVE

How many?

SIX

Like seventy-eight.

FIVE

You actually keep count?

SIX

Eyup.

FIVE

What do you do with your white friends?

SIX

Go to the mall, eat biscotti, play video games.

FIVE

For real?

SIX

Yeah. Why you making such a big deal? I do the same thing with them I do with anyone else.

FIVE

For real?

SIX

Eyup.

FIVE

Go to their houses?

SIX

Eyup.

FIVE

What do you do there?

SIX

We watch movies. About elephants.

FIVE

Do you talk?

SIX

Only when the channel needs to be changed.

FIVE

O. That sounds normal.

SIX

And when my friend reaches down for a bit of popcorn but accidentally eats a bit of my finger.

FIVE

Say what?

SIX

Sometimes she eats but doesn't realize she's eating me, so I'll be like, "Hey, Katelyn. You're eating me." If she hears me, she stops.

FIVE

O. That sounds normal.

SEVEN

Am
Am I?
Y'all, am I d— *(He would've said "dead.")*

FOUR

Black people

ALL

Yeah.

FOUR

Black people

ALL

Yeah.

FOUR

Black people

ALL

Yeah!

FOUR

We're gonna get in so much trouble for being gathered together like this, Black people

ALL

Yeah.

FOUR

And we ain't even in church, Black people

ALL

Yeah.

FOUR

And yelling, Black people

ALL

Yeah.

FOUR

And mad in public, Black people

ALL

Yeah.

FOUR

They might drop a nuke, Black people

ALL

Yeah.

FOUR

In fact, I'm sure they are, Black people

ALL

Yeah.

FOUR

I can hear the bomb coming.
You'd better leave something behind before it gets here!
Drop somethin!

(Four and/or Three and/or anyone else with shredded paper drops some.)

THREE

They're all like, "What's the problem, *(Inserts own name)*?"
'Cause as far as they're concerned, there isn't one.
Which of course is a little maddening.
I mean, just talking about it makes me feel like I'm orbiting them.
I don't want to orbit. I don't want to orbit.
What are they, the Sun? O god, it is maddening.
I tried to love, I tried.
It was like falling and waiting for the bottom
waiting for the bottom
You know it's going to come
But when?

SEVEN

O, shit.
There's someone
someone's behind me Shit.
following me?

(Seven walks swiftly to escape his pursuer.)

FIVE

But . . .

SIX

But?

FIVE

But what if she doesn't hear you?

SIX

Who? My friend?

FIVE

Yeah, what if your friend doesn't hear you say, "Hey, Katelyn. You're eating me," and doesn't stop eating you. What do you do next?

SIX

Well.
I usually just eat a little of myself. So she doesn't feel embarrassed.

FIVE

O.

SIX

Just a little of myself, you know?

FIVE

Yeah. Okay. That sounds normal—

SEVEN

O, he's definitely following me.
Definitely.

EIGHT

You ever get your neck fixed?

FOUR

No. But now the world is bent too, so it all evens out.

EIGHT

Damn.

SEVEN

But I don't know why he's following me.
I got this Y in me
This deep Y in me
I look like one of the dead ones
I might *be* one of the . . . so I don't know what else he want—

THREE

I tried. Try. Past and present. I mean, I really, really do and did.
I beam, I smile, I listen. I do not take offense.
This is an office function, after all.
This is a classroom, after all.
This is a production meeting, after all—

SEVEN

I don't know what else he want.
I don't know what else he want—

THREE

This is a play, after all—

SEVEN

Iss enough ghosts up in here—

(All take an audible breath and rush into the margins, save for Two.)

THIRD MOVEMENT

This third time around, all action occurs a bit more quickly than the last time. Damn near breakneck speed.

TWO

The People are coming because it is the day after or the day before it has gone down.
You know what I mean by "it," right?
The shit that don't stop.
It is the year *(Insert date and year)* and we are right here at *(Name of venue)* on stolen *(Name of Indigenous peoples who once held the land)* land.
and it is September 10th, 2014 in Utah, the questions still looming
And June 17th, 2015 in Charleston, the bodies still smoking
And July 5th, 2016, the boy still wailing for his daddy
And July 6th, 2016, the moan moaning and the red stain staining
And July 20th, 2018, the papa still pleading
And March 13th, 2020, the walls still smoking
And May 25th, 2020, the man still calling for his mama
And today, the people still trying to be people when it seems it might be easier to be something else.
Get it?
Bang!

EIGHT

MAMA WHERE'D YOU HIDE THAT ROSEBUSH
DADDY WHY'D YOU SINK THAT SHIP
I GOT NOTHIN TO PUT IN MY JEWELRY BOX
AND I'M FEELIN A LITTLE SICK

ALL

O

MAMA WON'T YOU TAKE MY TEMPERATURE
DADDY WON'T YOU FILL THIS SCRIPT
TRYNA GET WELL, TRYNA GET WELL
BEFORE I ABSOLUTELY LOSE MY SHHHHHH

Shh sh sh
Shh sh sh
Shh sh sh

(The tempo of "Fixing Miss" this time around must be really fast, as if the players are acting on fast-forward. The characterizations are angrier and the most realistic we've seen them. We see and feel their frustration with having to repeat themselves.)

TWO

The People prepare—

MADE

"Fixing Miss:" Play within play.
Characters: Made. Fed up.

MAN

Man. Weary of the margins. At attention.

MISS

Miss enters. White. Jittery.

MAN

Whatchoo need?

MISS

Nothing from you. Liberated.

MAN

Needs me some purpose—

MISS

Not my problem.

MAN

Characters in plays need purpose.

MISS

Not my problem.

MAN

Prolly gonna die.

MISS

Sounds like an exaggeration.

MAN

No, I'm actually afraid that I'm going to die—

MISS

Not my problem, nor my fault. Liberated. Could use a seat, though.

MAN

He becomes a seat.

MISS

Miss sees the Help.
Who's that?

MAN

That's *(Insert name of actor portraying Made)*.

MISS

What's her deal?

MAN

She might be tired.

MISS

Of what?

MAN

Let's ask her.

MISS

You there, come here.

MADE

Made looks to the audience.
Who's she talking to?

MISS

Miss asks Driver,
Who's she talking to?

MAN

I don't know. Lotta ghosts around here—

MISS

Miss asks the Help who she's talking to.

MADE

No one. Everyone.

MISS

Come here.

MADE

I'm busy.

MISS

I said come here.

MADE

Okay. I'll come.
If you get my name right.

MISS

If I what?

MADE

Get my name right. What's my name?

MISS

How am I to know?

MADE

He just told you.

MISS

Did he?

MAN

I did.

MISS

Well. You must be *(Insert name of female cast member who is not playing Made. That cast member speaks up from wherever they are onstage).*

CAST MEMBER 1

No. That's me.

MISS

Uh, okay. Then you must be *(Insert name of another female cast member who is not playing Made. That cast member speaks from wherever they are onstage).*

CAST MEMBER 2

No, that's me.

MISS

Okay, then you're definitely *(Insert name of cast member portraying Man).*

MAN

No, that's me.

MISS

Well, hell's bells! How can I be expected to keep you all straight?

(Made slaps Miss.)

This parody is an insult to my—
(Made slaps Miss again)
How am I supposed to—
(Made slaps Miss again)
Understand my role in this—

(Made slaps Miss again.
This time, Miss feels the slap. She holds her cheek in disbelief, falling to the ground.
Then she rises dramatically, making a long trek across the space. She stumbles. Everyone watches. She catches her balance, continuing on. Eventually she turns to face everyone. The actor performs the following naturalistically—no heightening, lets go of Miss completely:)

I'd like to apologize on behalf of my entire race.
That's what you want, isn't it?
I am so fucking sorry that I was born white and that there is racism in the world and that you have to suffer through it, but what do you want me to do, huh? Huh? Give up my own life? Wade around miserably, feeling bad about a bunch of shit that

happened before I was even born?! Anyone? Does anyone have an actual answer or are we all just supposed to join in this grand pity party?
Or do you just wanna take what's mine?
(She laughs)
O yes, that's what you want, isn't it?
To put on my clothes and go into my office
and sit behind my desk and give the orders.
Then you wanna drive my car to the decent neighborhood I've lived in for years,
and you wanna park in the driveway of the house my daddy built with his brothers and uncles and grandfathers.
And you wanna put your feet up on the furniture.
Because everything I have
this job
this car
this house
is rightfully yours no matter how hard I worked for it, right?
R i g h t ?

(By the end of this monologue, the actor has become Miss again. Heightened. Much drama.)

MAN

(No "negro dialect") Man snaps his fingers *(Snap)* so Miss can see what's in the floorboards of what she thinks is her house.

(Miss looks around, eyes wide.)

A truth sneaks in

MISS

Miss looks here and there for the comfort of a fellow White.

(Miss looks here and there, melodramatically.)

Finding none, she stumbles
falls
gets back up
stumbles and falls again
Then, the light catching her hair, she turns to the people she's always done her best to help and says:

(Miss turns to Man and Made. She is dying.)

There's
got to be
a
better way
for you
to protest than—

MADE

Nope.

(Miss is dead.)

MAN

She dead for good?

MADE

Nah. I give her about fifteen minutes.

(Three enters from the margins, moving through the space, dropping more paper.)

THREE

I am carrying my mother's things.
They are not mine—I mean they are not mine alone.
They are mine plus hers
They are seventy percent mine and thirty percent hers.

I carry them because her hands too shaky
I carry them because her arms too busy
I carry them because—
because them carry I
busy too arms her because them carry I
shaky too hands her because them carry I
hers percent thirty and mine percent seventy are they
hers plus mine are they
alone mine not are they—mean I mine not are they
things mother's my carrying am I—

(Seven enters. He's still being followed and terrified.)

SEVEN

He's coming fast, y'all.
He's right up on me but
I don't
I don't know him
And I ain't steal nothin
I swear I ain't
Wait
I do
Maybe I do know him
He looks kinda familiar—

(And Seven is on the run again. One, Eight and Four enter and sprinkle more paper on the ground, preparing. Five and Six speak:)

FIVE

I gotta say, though,
I once knew a dude whose friend could never hear him when he said, "You're eating me."
So he kept on eating himself alongside his friend so the friend wouldn't get embarrassed, you know?

SIX

Yeah? What happened?

FIVE

He ate himself all the way down to just a mouth and a throat.

SIX

O shit. What'd his friend do?

FIVE

She didn't notice.

SIX

O. That sounds normal.

SEVEN

He's coming faster
He got a look in his eyes like he—

THREE

I am carrying my sister's things
They are not mine—or rather they are not mine alone
They are mine plus hers
Her palms too dry
her head too full
I am carrying my brother's things
They are not mine—or rather they are not mine alone
They are mine plus his
They are seventy percent mine and thirty percent his
I carry them because his chest too mouth too slack too riddled
too big too brawny too tight too much to handle to do
too bad too bad too bad
too bad too bad too bad
This is my face.

This is the face that I have.
It is a pretty good face, don't you think?
No. Don't answer that.
This is my face
The one I was given when faces were being given out
The job of a face is to tell the outside what the inside is thinking
Or to hide what the inside is thinking from the outside
Is that not the job of a face?
And if it is, is my face doing its job?

EIGHT AND FOUR

Don't answer that.
This is my face.
My mother pulled it from her ribs
ironed it, shined it, and here it is.
A bit too much starch but Mom did what she had to do.

FIVE AND SIX

This is my face. It is kind of soggy because my father thinks it is a handkerchief. He cried into it when his mother died. I can't get it dry. I can't get it dry.

SEVEN

He's
y'all
He won't stop
Y'all he won't—

TWO

BANG

(Seven falls, dead. A moment of horrified stillness as they look at Seven, who has fallen on the ground, now cushioned by what should be lots of shredded white paper.)

MADE

Made doesn't have any kids
Made doesn't have any kids and it is after the boy's been filled with holes
the body washed and sobbed over
and hymned over and placed into the ground.
It is when the news cycle has cycled and
his name has gone cold on nearly everyone's tongue.
It is evening time and Made stands grinding glass
and wishing
She wishes she'd had The Talk with her son.
She wishes she'd sat him down
placed a firm hand on his shoulder and said:
Son,
When a white boy says, "Don't worry, you'll be clean like me some day."
Find the nearest pile of dog shit
and rub his miserable face in it.
When a white woman crosses the street because she sees you coming
Laugh maniacally. Give that bitch somethin to run away from.

When white folks call the police on you for just standing there
for merely being in time and space
reach into their chests, pull their hearts out
and eat them.

Made wishes, Made wishes.

When you've had a seizure on a train and an old white man in a suit
drags you onto the platform so he won't be delayed getting home
Wake your ass up
put your hands around his throat
and put that motherfucker on the tracks
See if that get him home faster

When you're minding your own business and some monster stabs you in the neck
Go ahead and die, baby. Die easy.
But then I want you to come back in thirty days
and when you find him
skin him alive
strip by strip of skin
Take your time
I wantcha to do it s t r a t e g i c a l l y
Do his eyelids first
so he get to watch
'Cause they ain't learnin. You throwin words but it ain't working.
You marchin, you screaming through a bullhorn but you dead
and they smilin and I can't have it. I can't have it no more

Made wishes O Made wishes
and she grinds that glass
and she burns and she burns and she burns
O god
She burns.

(Made sees the others around her.)

But

there's a whole lotta ghosts up in here
spirits in the margins lookin at Made
lookin at me like they think
I should turn back
Give you less things to destroy
It's nothing personal, I swear.
I'm just a bit tired of your face lookin like it be lookin.
It's everywhere.
On my coffee mug. Over my shoulder. In my cereal. In my shoes.

On my chest.
Headlining my newspaper
Everywhere, everywhere.

(During the following, all circle Seven's body, building the intensity of their movements and voices.)

ONE AND TWO

Comin outta my headphones sounding but not looking like me. On every screen. On every screen. On every screen. In the thread count of my sheets. At the beginning of this sentence.

ONE, TWO, THREE AND FOUR

Where the sidewalk ends. On the moon. On my soft palate. Down the street. Up the block. In my secrets. All up in the tofu. In Egypt. Overhead in a chopper. At the front of the submarine. In both the blockbuster and the flop. On the board. Treading the boards. In the dictionary. In the thesaurus.

ONE, TWO, THREE, FOUR, FIVE AND SIX

In the essay. In the footnote. In my uterus. Folded into my wallet. On the time stamp. In the credits. On the dotted line. Under my dick. On the bumper of my car. In the crease of my inner arm. In the promise. At the start and finish lines.

ONE, TWO, THREE, FOUR, FIVE, SIX AND EIGHT

On the beach. On the brochure. In my spit. In the ozone. On the dirt road. In my dreams (both day and regular). Past the stop sign. Behind the war zone. In the map key. Next door to the salon. In the mayoral race. On the court. In the court. Where my lips are split. Picking up the crumbs. In satellite. In stereo. En route. In season (always). In the season consistently. In the musculature. In the tremor and the sucked teeth. In Mama's blues. In Daddy's screams. In the mirror and so I must close the door on you.

(All give a group yell. Expulsion, expansion, cleansing of the spirit and the space. This takes as long as it needs to. Four waits for it to die out before they speak. By now they're in a tight circle around Seven's body.)

FOUR

The people speak the names.

(Four goes to each participant in the circle individually with a bowl filled with small pieces of red ribbon. Each participant, save for Seven, recites the following:)

PARTICIPANT

"My name is *(Name of participant)*. I send something up in the name of *(Name of someone lost to racialized violence)* who was born on *(Birthdate of lost one)* and taken away on *(Date lost one was murdered)*."

(The participant takes two handfuls of the red ribbon.)

FOUR

Black people

ALL OTHERS

Yeah

FOUR

Black people

ALL OTHERS

Yeah

FOUR

Speak the names

(All speak the name of the lost one they're honoring in unison.)

Speak the names.

(All speak the name of the lost one they're honoring in unison.)

May they what?

ALL OTHERS

Rest in power.

FOUR

May they what?

ALL OTHERS

Rest in power.

FOUR

Black people

ALL OTHERS

Yeah

FOUR

Drop somethin.
Black people

ALL OTHERS

Yeah

FOUR

Drop somethin.

(All slowly and silently let the ribbon fall from their hands and onto Seven's body. An offering. When all of the ribbon has been dropped . . .)

Black people

ALL OTHERS

Yeah

FOUR

They will call this a riot

ALL OTHERS

Yeah

FOUR

They will call this a riot

ALL OTHERS

Yeah

FOUR

What a riot.

ALL OTHERS

(Spoken, sarcasm) Ha ha ha

FOUR

What a riot

ALL OTHERS

Ha ha ha

FOUR

Black people

ALL OTHERS

Yeah

FOUR

Get quiet.

The people are quiet for a full minute to honor the dead.

(All are still for a full minute. Respect this full minute. They help Seven to stand and join the circle.)

You mad?

ONE

Ah!

FOUR

You mad?

TWO

Ah!

FOUR

You mad?

THREE

Ah!

FOUR

You mad?

FIVE

Ah!

FOUR

You mad?

SIX

Ah!

FOUR

You mad?

EIGHT

Ah!

FOUR

You mad?

SEVEN

Ah!

FOUR

Black people.

ALL OTHERS

Yeah!

FOUR

Black people.

ALL OTHERS

Yeah.

FOUR

You mad?

ALL

Ah!

FOUR

You mad?

ALL

Ah!

FOUR

You mad?

(The following song/chant is confrontational. The participants address the viewers and maybe move into the audience.)

ALL

WHO ME?
I'M NOT MAD AT ALL
I'M DRESSED TO THE NINES
AND I'M GOIN TO A BALL

WHAT'S THAT?
THAT'S WHERE MY PEOPLE STAY
WE INSIDE, WE OUTSIDE, WE THERE
WE ON THE WAY

TO WHAT?
TO WHAT IT'S GONNA BE
THE MESS AND THE MESSAGE
THE PEOPLE IN THE STREETS

WE FALLIN WE STANDING
WE DANCIN IN THE LIGHT
WE KICKIN, WE RUNNIN
WE PLAYIN AND WE FIGHT LIKE

DOO DOO DOO DOO
DOO DOO DOO DOO

AH AH AH AH
AH AH AH AH

(All return to the playing space and stand in a circle.)

FOUR

Black people.

ALL OTHERS

Yeah.

FOUR

Send it up!

Send it up!

Send it up!

(They send it up. This is a rigorous movement to rid the body/spirit of things that need ridding. Like shaking off a haint. Like a self-exorcism. The participants should take all the time this needs. When this dies down, Eight sings a solo:)

EIGHT

ONE DAY I'M GON PUT ON MY BEST SHOES
ONE DAY I'M GON PUT ON MY BEST SHOES
ONE DAY I'M GON PUT ON MY BEST SHOES
AND SET MY FEET TO WALKIN
ONE DAY I'M GON PUT ON MY BEST SHOES

ONE DAY I'M GON CUT OFF ALL MY HAIR
ONE DAY I'M GON CUT OFF ALL MY HAIR
ONE DAY I'M GON CUT OFF ALL MY HAIR
AND NEVER MIND THEM WATCHING
ONE DAY I'M GON CUT OFF ALL MY HAIR

ONE DAY I'M GON SEE YOU STANDING THERE
ONE DAY I'M GON SEE YOU STANDING THERE
ONE DAY I'M GON SEE YOU STANDING THERE
I HOPE YOU KNOW YOU KNOW ME
ONE DAY I'M GON SEE YOU STANDING THERE

ALL

ONE DAY I'M GON LOOK UP TO THE SKY
ONE DAY I'M GON LOOK UP TO THE SKY

ONE DAY I'M GON LOOK UP TO THE SKY
AND FIND IT WON'T BE FALLING
ONE DAY I'M GON LOOK UP TO THE SKY

HEY Y'ALL
HEY
HEY Y'ALL
HEY
HEY Y'ALL HEY Y'ALL HEY Y'ALL HEY

(During the course of the "HEY Y'ALL" portion of the song, each person takes turns taking space and dancing in the center of the circle. This is joyful. Once everyone has had their turn, they return to seriousness. Two addresses us:)

TWO

The people are going because it is time.
The people are going because it is time but before they do,
Earlier, many of you wrote some things down you'd like to offer to Black people.
I'd like to share a few of them now for anyone present
and send them up to those no longer with us. Please sit forward in your chair and plant your feet as we do this.

(Someone hands Two a few of the notes written in the beginning of the ritual. It's probably best to screen these.)

I'll read what's written and we'll all repeat it, sending it up.
Here we go.

(Two reads three notes and asks the audience to repeat them three times each.)

We've all seen, heard, and experienced a lot this evening.

(Takes time to look around the room, giving people a moment.)

As we think about these things, let's take a collective breath. Please join us if you need to. On three: One, two, three.

(They breathe.)

Again.

(Breath.)

And one last time

(Breath.)

The ritual is not over
In a minute we'll disperse for the final portion
But, these are our last few moments together as one group
so we want to thank you.

(They gather for bows as he speaks.)

We want to thank you
we want to thank you for being here with us.

(Bows.)

At this time, we'd like to invite the Black folks who are present to stay in this space and we invite our non-Black friends to head out into the lobby where someone is waiting to greet you. We'll take just a very few minutes to do this and we'll continue

(To the Black folxs, in their space:)

Let's form a circle.

If there is anyone here who would like to speak the name of someone we've lost to anti-Black violence, please take a step forward.

(People may step forward to speak a name. Allow as much or as little time for this as necessary.)

Let's form a circle together.
We're gonna take a moment just to be with each other.
Look at the face of each person in this circle.

(This happens.)

The idea that we're separate is an illusion.
Racism will make you feel lonely but no one here is alone.
We've got a strong tradition of community.
We've got each other
And
We've got the ghosts, the ancestors in the margins rooting for us.

Now I'm gonna give some calls and I'd love for y'all to respond with "yeah."

Black people
Yeah
Black people
Yeah
Black people
Yeah
You Beautiful people
Yeah
You Creative people
Yeah
You Strong people
Yeah
You Tender people

Yeah
You Smart people
Yeah
You Funny people
Yeah
You Varied people
Yeah
You Fly people
Yeah
You Sky people
Yeah
You Dark-skinned people
Yeah
You Light-skinned people
Yeah
You Middle-of-the-Road Brown people
Yeah
You Passing people
Yeah
You Queer people
Yeah
You Black Panther people
Yeah
You Blues people
Yeah
You Quiet people
Yeah
You Book-Read people
Yeah
You Hood people
Yeah
You Field Holler people
Yeah
You Trans people
Yeah

You Ancient people
Yeah
There is love, Black people
Yeah
There is love, Black people
Yeah
Right here, Black people
Yeah
Do you feel it, Black people?
Yeah
Do you feel it, Black people?
Yeah
You are here, Black people
Yeah
You are here, Black people
Yeah
And you belong, Black people
Yeah.

Thank you all so much for being with us.
We hope this has been useful to you.
We invite you to head out into the lobby where we hope you'll keep the conversation going.

(Meanwhile, a facilitator reads the following to the non-Black audience members once they've made their way into a separate space.)

FACILITATOR

The following is a note from the creator of *What to Send Up When It Goes Down*:
"A good friend once told me that we each have a different job where challenging racism is concerned. She spoke to the ways she could use her privilege as a white woman to dismantle the white supremacist ideology that contributes to the deaths of so many people.

As a Black woman and writer, I am uniquely positioned to create a piece of theater focused on making space for Black people. This is one way I can contribute. This is my offering.

I'd like to end this ritual by challenging you to consider what *you* are uniquely positioned to offer. As a non-Black person, what is a tangible way you can disrupt the idea responsible for all of these lives needlessly taken?

My hope is that you will consider this deeply.

My further hope is that your consideration will turn to action."

END

ALESHEA HARRIS's *Is God Is* (directed by Taibi Magar at Soho Rep. and Ola Ince at The Royal Court Theatre) won the Relentless Award and an Obie Award. *What to Send Up When It Goes Down* (directed by Whitney White, produced by The Movement Theatre Company, BAM, and Playwrights Horizons) was featured in the April 2019 issue of *American Theatre* magazine and received a special commendation from the Susan Smith Blackburn Prize. Harris's awards include the Windham-Campbell Prize, the Steinberg Playwright Award, the Hermitage Greenfield Prize, and The Horton Foote Prize.

Theatre Communications Group would like to offer our special thanks to Judith O. Rubin for her generous support of the publication of Is God Is/What to Send Up When It Goes Down *by Aleshea Harris*

JUDITH O. RUBIN is Chairman of the Board of Playwrights Horizons and TCG's National Council for the American Theatre. She is a member of the Tony Awards Administration Committee, the Laurents/Hatcher Foundation, the Mount Sinai Health System, and the New York Community Trust. She has served on the NEA's National Council on the Arts, the New York State Council on the Arts and Board of Regents, as president of 92nd Street Y, and as a trustee of TCG and Public Radio International.

TCG books sponsored by Judith O. Rubin include:

The Antipodes by Annie Baker
The Flick by Annie Baker
Is God Is / What to Send Up When It Goes Down by Aleshea Harris
A Strange Loop by Michael R. Jackson

THEATRE COMMUNICATIONS GROUP's mission is to lead for a just and thriving theatre ecology. Through its Core Values of Activism, Artistry, Diversity, and Global Citizenship, TCG advances a better world for theatre and a better world because of theatre. TCG Books is the largest independent trade publisher of dramatic literature in North America, with 18 Pulitzer Prizes for Best Play on its book list. The book program commits to the life-long career of its playwrights, keeping all of their plays in print. TCG Books' other authors include: Nilo Cruz, Jackie Sibblies Drury, Athol Fugard, Jeremy O'Harris, Quiara Alegría Hudes, David Henry Hwang, Branden Jacobs-Jenkins, The Kilroys, Tony Kushner, Young Jean Lee, Tracy Letts, Lynn Nottage, Dael Orlandersmith, Suzan-Lori Parks, Sarah Ruhl, Stephen Sondheim, Paula Vogel, Anne Washburn, and August Wilson, among many others.

Support TCG's work in the theatre field by becoming a member or donor: www.tcg.org

tcg